Teen Quiet Times

By
MARGARET GRAHAM

MOODY PRESS · Chicago

To
Gertrude Earehart Uding,
one of God's faithful "helps,"
1 Corinthians 12:28

ISBN: 0-8024-6860-8

ACKNOWLEDGMENT

These devotionals originally appeared as "Talking with Teens," weekly features for the senior high paper, *My Delight,* published by Union Gospel Press, Cleveland, Ohio.

1

Rebels

Every generation has produced its own rebels. Surprisingly, much of the good that has been accomplished in the world has been done by those who dared to stand for their convictions. But the majority of the present rebels seem to differ from the rest of society only because they enjoy being different. Either they want to be identified with those who will accomplish purposes, or they want attention.

Henry Thoreau was a rebel of sorts—or an eccentric. He quit civilization for two years and lived in a cabin by Walden's pond. He decided that he could work six weeks in a year and provide for his basic needs. He kept his possessions to the barest necessities.

One time he refused to pay his taxes because he was opposed to this government's support of slavery and the war to annex Texas. He was jailed overnight until someone bailed him out. From this experience came his essay on the right to dissent.

Today, eccentrics of all kinds quote Thoreau. But seldom does anyone examine the Scripture to see if Thoreau's ideas are according to God's Word. Furthermore, the Lord Jesus Christ certainly set an example in the affairs of men and gave us many concrete reasons for Christian behavior.

There is no question but that Jesus was considered a revolutionary. He had a lot to say that was contrary to the religious tradition of His day. He extended religion to the motives and attitude of the heart rather than to mere observance of outward acts. When you consider the religious establishment of His day, you can easily understand why they executed Him. He went contrary to all that they taught and practiced!

Yet our Lord never took it upon Himself to reform the Roman government. He said that we should render to government (even a tyrannical government such as Rome) the things required of good citizens, and render to God the things that belong to God. He never led protest marches or demonstrated against social evils, but He got at the heart of the matter—individual hearts.

We may draw certain principles from our Lord's example to apply to our own situation although we live in a free society and He lived in a dictator's society. Jesus used the abuses of the system in which He lived to demonstrate the love of God. For instance, it was a law that a Roman soldier could require another person to carry his pack for a mile, but he could not require him to carry it further. Jesus taught that a believer should be willing to carry the pack for the "second mile." Why? To be servants? Not only that, but to show graciousness. Didn't He wash other men's feet? Are His disciples above their Lord? Remember that Jesus said, "Learn of Me."

4

2

Bashfulness

Are you shy? Are you sensitive? Take heart, you might very well be a very refreshing person! Who likes a talkative person who never says anything?

Many children are afraid of strange people. When visitors come, they hide because they are shy. Sooner or later they outgrow this, but sometimes the process is very painful.

Some shy people are shy because they take themselves too seriously. They exaggerate how much people really think about them. Others are shy because they were often embarrassed as children.

Seldom is a shy person self-conscious in all kinds of situations. One who may find it difficult to walk into a room full of people may, nevertheless, have no stage fright in addressing an audience. To get at the root of your problem, it is important to try to figure out why certain situations cause you to freeze up.

Our Lord can use you better if you can meet all kinds of people gracefully and if you can carry on an intelligent conversation. As a witness for Christ you cannot afford to be boring. Our Lord attracted multitudes, not merely by what is commonly termed "personality" but by the fact that His character was revealed by what He said and did.

If you are ill at ease in meeting strangers, it will help you to learn how to introduce people and how to be introduced. A book on etiquette from the library will solve this problem. Or, ask someone to teach you who knows the proper thing to do.

If you can never think of anything to say, listen to what other people talk about for clues. You might be surprised to learn that most people do not carry on learned conversations. They talk about sports, hobbies, travel, people, clothes, church, school, or their jobs. Boys like to talk about cars, girls about friends.

The best conversationalists are those who can ask a leading question so that the other person will talk about himself or his interests. People are always more interested in themselves than in you, so steer the conversation toward their family, friends, experiences, likes, and dislikes. Be a good listener but comment enough to be interesting.

Your appearance will help you to relax. Make sure that you look your best at all times. If your clothes are neat and you feel confident that you look nice, you can concentrate on being entertaining. Feeling bashful is a handicap that anyone can overcome if he will make a definite effort to do so.

3

"The Negro Pasteur"

Few men have had the obstacles to overcome that George Washington Carver had, yet few men have achieved as much. Born a slave in Diamond, Missouri, in 1864, he was sickly from birth. However, when he was quite young he had an intense interest in plants.

He desperately wanted an education but there were no schools in his area that accepted Negroes. He had to leave home to find a school. After he had learned all that the teacher could teach him, he would move on to another school. Then came the day when he had to find a college. Because of his unusual intelligence, he was at last successful.

From college George went to the Tuskegee Institute, a Negro school in the South. He spent the rest of his life there, discovering new foods and crops for the poor. He found that 300 products could be made from the peanut alone.

His work earned him the titles of "The Peanut Man" and "The Negro Pasteur." In 1947 the United States Post Office issued a stamp bearing his picture, and his birthplace was made a national monument.

Although many honors were heaped upon him, Dr. Carver always gave all glory to God, for he had accepted Christ as his Saviour when he was young. He used to tell this story: "When I was young, I said to God, 'Lord, tell me the mystery of the universe.' But God answered, 'That knowledge is reserved for Me alone.' So I said, 'Lord, tell me the mystery of the peanut.' Then the Lord said, 'Well, George, that's more nearly your size.' And He told me."

Once when he was brought before a group of statesmen and scientists to explain his peanut products, Dr. Carver was asked where he learned so much. He pointed to his old worn Bible. The group was astonished. "There is nothing about a peanut in the Bible!" they said. Dr. Carver answered, "No, but the God of the peanut is there."

4

Continue in Prayer

No subject is emphasized more in the Bible than prayer. There are repeated commands and repeated promises concerning prayer. In Genesis we read, "Then began men to call upon the name of the Lord," and at the end of the Bible we read, "Amen." Daniel prayed three times a day, and some of his prayers are recorded in Scripture, as are the prayers of David, Elijah, and others.

Anything that God has made prominent in His Word should be made conspicuous in the life of the Christian. The Lord considered our need for prayer to be paramount. Do you? If not, you are ignorant of your poverty. "Hast thou no mercy to ask of God?" Spurgeon asked. "Then, may the Lord's mercy show thee thy misery. A prayerless soul is a Christless soul."

In John Bunyan's allegory of Mansoul, he tells of a time when the Prince Emmanuel (Christ) had left Mansoul because they were feasting at the table of Mr. Carnal Security. When the citizens of Mansoul were questioned by Mr. Godly Fear, they could not recall when the Prince had left.

So it is with Christians today who go along in their own strength, getting by on their talents, ignoring fellowship with Christ. They cannot remember when fellowship was broken!

The citizens of Mansoul repented and sent messages to the Prince through the Lord High Secretary (the Holy Spirit), but they had to wait a long time before they realized that fellowship had been restored.

It is this waiting that is difficult. It is then that we are tempted to despair. But if we are patient we will come to realize that although we did not *feel* His presence, He was there all the time. Only God knows why He makes us wait. It is never too late to begin to "continue in prayer" (Col 4:2).

5

Cheers, Applause, and—

Do you ever show your appreciation for a performer by clapping? Do you ever cheer for a contestant or team? Of course you do. It is perfectly natural that a spectator would voice, or express in some way, his appreciation for what is going on. A fan feels that he is a vital part of the performance, because he knows that he cheers the spirits of those who are participating.

Christians are spectators, and even participants, in the performance of heaven itself. Isn't it the most natural thing in the world that they should voice their praise of almighty God when they see Him at work in the world?

Actually, it is not up to a Christian to choose whether he will praise God. The Lord deserves every Christian's praise. "Sing forth the honour of his name: make his praise glorious" (Ps 66:2). This law is written in our hearts, so that when we watch a crusade on television and witness hundreds of people indicating their acceptance of Christ, we cannot help but praise the Lord.

Not only on such special occasions should we praise the Lord, but we should do so continually—every day. If Christians do not show forth His praise, who will?

11

The doleful Christian, the one who is always down-hearted, is guilty of dishonoring God. No amount of serving or proper behavior can discharge one's duty to praise.

Satan attempts to keep us from praise, but certain positive steps can insure the Lord's praise. Let His praise be your first thought upon awaking. At lunch-time, voice a word of praise. At the setting of sun and at bedtime, let your grateful heart express itself.

Perhaps you wonder how a person can think of enough to praise God for without becoming monot-onously repetitious. There is nothing wrong with repetition if it is heartfelt, but subjects for praise are as varied as the colors of a kaleidoscope. Read the Psalms to see why others praised God. Read hymns and the stories behind the hymns. Soon you will be reminded a hundred times a day of the greatness of God, and you will discover that praising God does something for you!

Of all the characters in the Bible, which one praised God most? That's right—David. Of all the characters in the Bible, which one is described by the Lord as "a man after mine own heart"? That's right—David. If you would be godly, begin by increasing your praise of God.

6

When God Seems Far Away

Did you ever try desperately to "get through to God" but failed? You examined your life to see if sin was the hindrance and you confessed everything you knew to be wrong—even straightened out everything between yourself and others. Still there was no satisfaction in your praying. No verse of Scripture came to assure you that you were in God's good grace and that you were heard.

Take heart! This may be a subtle trick of Satan. He is probably badgering you to keep testing your *feelings* rather than to accept by faith the promises of God.

If you want to see a fellow who really *felt* secure, look at the rich fool. He said, "Soul, you have many goods laid up for many years to come; take your ease, eat, drink and be merry" (Lk 12:19, NASB). He felt as if he didn't have a care in the world.

The rich fool was apparently an unbeliever, but professing Christians often have the same false sense of well-being. The church people at Laodicea said, "I am rich, and increased with goods, and have need of nothing," but the Lord said that they knew not that they were "wretched, and miserable, and poor, and blind, and naked" (Rev 3:17).

If you feel a bit miserable, at least you are not in the spiritual condition of the Laodiceans or the rich fool.

If you have done your part you may rest assured that God is doing His part. Accept by faith the fact that He is hearing you and that the answers you seek will be found.

A secretary was asked what she does when she experiences a period of spiritual drought, a time when there seems to be no response from God. She said, "I go in the boss's office, close the door, and sit down at his desk. Then I praise the Lord and recall the many attributes of His person. I thank Him for all that He has done for me throughout my life. It isn't important that I feel His presence or have any particular emotion; it is enough that we understand each other."

> Jesus, I am resting, resting
> In the joy of what Thou art.

How the devil would like to have us continually taking our spiritual pulse like the hypochondriac of medical fame! How he delights in having us so concerned with our spiritual aches and pains that we cannot be absorbed in worship or service to Christ. How diligently he seeks to have us disturbed so that we are paralyzed spiritually.

7

Comparing Experience

Do you ever compare yourself with other Christians and become confused because the Lord does not deal with you as He does with someone else?

Arch, a young man in prep school, often heard his classmates testify that when they needed money they would pray and in time a check would be received. Arch said that when he needed money, he prayed about it but usually his answer came in the form of an extra job to do.

A young girl in Bible school asked the Lord to give her some needed spending money. That night some-one called and asked her to go to a strange, large city to baby-sit. She was afraid to go to the big hotel on the city street, but the work was God's way of giving her the money she needed.

Do not be confused if the testimonies of other Christians differ from your experience. As you read of Daniel being spared from the lions, you should also be aware that God permitted the early Christians in Rome to be devoured by wild beasts in the arena.

Peter was delivered by an angel from prison, but Stephen was stoned to death. Elijah was fed by ravens by the brook Cherith, but do not forget poor Job and all his sufferings.

Moses met God on Mount Sinai, but David, a man after God's own heart, never had a vision of Him. Jacob was a cheat and a rascal, yet God spoke to him and showed him a ladder that reached to heaven.

Such wonderful experiences are not based on how good a person is, but strictly upon God's choice. God does not have to reveal Himself in any particular way at all times. Christian experience is as varied as the recorded histories of Bible characters. Do not insist that someone else must have the same or similar experiences as you have. God deals with His children as individuals.

In the variety of ways that He deals with us, we see many different aspects of His mercy and character. How dull it would be if we only saw God in one light, or in one way of dealing with mankind. Yet, there are Christians who would like to narrow God to one way of working. They set up patterns to measure one's spirituality. God does not offer such oversimplification. Only He can judge the heart of the believer; therefore, only He can rightly judge who is spiritual and who is not.

Trust the Lord, who bought you to "perfect that which concerneth," you, and do not measure your Christianity by someone else's experience.

8

Blanket Decisions

By "blanket decisions" is meant making a decision to cover a wide cross section of right or wrong things. Instead of analyzing the right or wrong of an individual practice, a person might decide against or for a group. Take, for example, sports. To make things easy for himself, one might say, "Sports are good; therefore I will enjoy *all* sports." A Christian could make serious mistakes in such a decision. There are brutal sports that risk lives. Can a Christian approve of such sports in the light of God's Word? Hardly, but that does not mean that there are not wholesome sports that he may enjoy.

Certain television programs may be acceptable whereas others are not. Certain companions may be good and others bad. How is a Christian to discern?

According to God's Word, a Christian should honestly ask, "Is it wrong?" If it violates any of the commandments or principles laid down in the Bible, it must be rejected.

Second, he should ask, "Can I do it to the glory of God?" If there is no benefit to anyone, how can it be to the glory of God?

Third, "Will it cost me part of my eternal reward?" Doing that which is "good" may be the enemy of doing that which is "best." If you choose television above a prayer meeting, you choose wrongly.

Fourth, "Will it injure a weak brother or cause him grief?" You may be helped by a certain practice; but if a weak Christian would be harmed by your example, you must refrain from it.

Fifth, "Is my conscience clear about it?" Unfortunately, we have a way of getting conscience to agree with much of what we want to do. Conscience is not a reliable guide for that reason. However, if your conscience hurts, it is likely that your choice is wrong.

Sixth, "Does it make for harmony and help others?" If what you enjoy distresses someone else—parents, friends or neighbors—you should reevaluate it. A practice that causes division among God's people is especially wrong.

Seventh, "Does Christian love permit it?" Spurgeon once wrote, "It is a great sin to love a little sin." If we love the satisfaction of a practice more than we love the brethren, we are guilty.

Do you recognize sin when you see it? Many Christians do not. Some who do recognize sin don't have the will to forsake it. Remember, even a very small leak can sink a large ship. So it is with sin in the Christian life. Read 1 Corinthians 8:1—11:1 for some identifying marks of sin. Ask the Holy Spirit to make you sensitive to the sin areas in your life, and then, make a blanket decision to hate all sin and get rid of it.

9

You Can't Win Them All!

Who says you can't win them all? Oh, yes, the fans tell you that, after a game when your team loses. Even the coach might say it to make you feel better. Maybe it is true in baseball, but is it true in life?

The Bible says the Christian is supposed to be a winner. In the Revelation, Jesus told each of the seven churches that the ones who "overcome" are the ones who will enter heaven.

There is no excuse for a Christian to be defeated in his personal life. The Lord promises to supply all our need according to His riches in glory. Circumstances do not have to get us down because we are told, "My grace is sufficient for thee: for my strength is made perfect in weakness" (2 Co 12:9).

Don't accept the attitude, "You can't win them all," because you *can* win. In Romans we are told that we are more than conquerors through Him who loves us.

Why do you sometimes fail? Isn't it because you try to do things in your own strength? God never promised that you would be able to overcome temptation nor win victories by your own willpower. Jesus said, "All power is given unto me." Every day we must acknowledge the fact that without Him we can do nothing, but, as Paul claimed, through Christ we can do all things.

How does spiritual power relate to such things as passing a French test? An unbeliever can pass a French test without any reliance upon God. However, the Christian knows that his normal mind as well as his allotment of time for study and preparation are gifts from God. He is utterly dependent upon God for these necessary factors. More than that, he can ask the Lord to quicken his mind so that he can learn more easily. He can ask for the stick-to-itiveness to study effectively.

Does this guarantee that he will pass French? Not necessarily. God may have a purpose in his failing a subject. There are spiritual values in that kind of failing—lessons to be learned—corrections to be made. Personal victory is in knowing how to accept a failure in a manner pleasing to God.

In this sense a Christian can win them all.

Mary was a splendid Christian girl who studied hard and who prayed hard, but she could not do well in school. This was a problem to her, but the Lord used her attitude as a witness to what He can do in a believer's life. Her efforts were recognized by her teachers and fellow students, and they were impressed by her sweetness when she was disappointed. They knew without being told that Mary had something others do not have. She really was a winner!

10

Individual Vs. Church

Today there seems to be an emphasis upon one's individual relationship with the Lord rather than the blessing of all the members of Christ's body. Sometimes this emphasis results in a kind of competition between Christians to determine which one is the most spiritual.

The Lord Jesus was concerned with the blessing of His entire church. When the apostle Paul was writing his letters to the churches, the Holy Spirit directed him to address the church as a whole.

It is true that an individual must walk closely with the Lord, but he should be aware of the needs of the whole church and of his local church in particular. In Hebrews we read the warning that a "root of bitterness" in a group or in an individual may "defile" many. The writer goes on to tell his readers to be on the alert lest a person commit fornication or profanity. We are, indeed, our "brother's keeper" in spiritual matters.

This does not mean that we should feel superiority over fellow Christians, but we should feel responsible for the spiritual life of the church. As Paul wrote, "We are members one of another."

As well as being concerned about possible weaknesses in the church, we should covet God's best for our fellow Christians. If we desire power, love, and joy in our own lives then we should equally desire these gifts for others.

To fulfill one's responsibility in the body of Christ, it is not well to criticize. It is far better to pray definitely about our concerns. Other than this, we can only set an example unless we are in a position of leadership.

Sins in the Christian life are caused by wrong attitudes toward God, toward circumstances, toward one's body, and toward spiritual realities. If we do not understand that we worship a holy and just God, we are likely to fall into contempt. If we do not see the hand of God at work in circumstances, we are likely to grumble and grow bitter. If we do not regard the body as the temple of the Holy Spirit, we are likely to succumb to sins of the flesh. If we do not keep eternal values in view, we will live a worldly and worthless life.

All these attitudes bear upon the testimony of the body of Christ. One of the greatest contributions that you can make to the life of the church is to straighten out your attitudes and to selflessly endeavor that the entire body of Christ be blessed.

11

Special Joys

What fun would it be to have a new hairdo if no one saw it? Would it be any fun to have a birthday if no one remembered it? All of us want recognition, and we want to share our special joys.

In your family, do you enter into the good fortune of your brothers and sisters? If your family doesn't care if you won the track meet or sold the most magazines, a great deal of the joy you might have felt was taken away from you,

You cannot do anything about those who do not share your successes and accomplishments, but you can do something about sharing those of other members of your family. If your father gets a raise in salary, why not plan a celebration? When your sister plays a solo in the band concert, get all the family to attend and treat her to a special joy.

Sometimes things happen at school that your parents do not know about, and your brothers and sisters are not likely to tell if it involves them and some accomplishment. Show your interest and pride by telling your folks.

Boasting is wrong; but within the family circle, there are some things that bind us together. One of them is pride in one another.

Instead of rejoicing in Jesus' works, His half brothers and sisters ridiculed Him. On one occasion they thought that He was crazy. Later, they saw their error, and two of them became leaders in the early church.

Family morale is important to happiness in the home. If we cannot show Christian love and interest to members of our own families, it is doubtful that we can show it to others. A little enthusiasm for what your family is and does can go a long way toward raising their morale. This is especially true in a family which has problems.

12

Remembered? For What?

A famous singer was asked by an interviewer, "How would you like to be remembered?"

The singer replied, "I would like to be remembered for singing in a new manner, for living my life of fun, and for having friends."

What about you? Of course, by the law of averages, you have many years ahead of you; but, in a sense, life is full of little "deaths" or separations. When you graduate from high school you will either enter college or take a position in the business world.

Sooner or later, you will probably leave home and marry. As a parent you will serve your family. You may be called into military service or Christian work in a foreign land. Life is full of changes. With each change you leave behind those who will remember you for the brief association you have shared.

How would you like to be remembered by your classmates? Perhaps you think you do not care or that no one will remember you. But you should care because you are Christ's representative to your classmates; it matters what others think of you, for it reflects, in some measure, what they think of Christ. You will be remembered, even if it's only for being shy and hard to get to know.

In years to come, your classmates will take down old yearbooks and point to your picture and make some kind of comment. The Lord will be glorified if the sight of your picture reminds them of Christ. "He was a fine Christian boy." "That was the girl who spoke to me about the Lord when my father died."

Someone has said that friends are like ships passing in the dark. That is, they are here for a short period of time, then gone. When you are enjoying a friendship you do not think about how soon your paths will separate.

The impression you make for the Lord on a friend can be a lifetime impression.

How do you want to be remembered by your family? Will you be thought of as the one who always brought a bit of cheer in the front door? As the one who acted as peacemaker in family disputes? The one who always went the second mile to be helpful? The one who cared enough about the rest of the family to make personal sacrifices of pleasure or comfort?

Even the Lord has a "book of remembrance." In Malachi we read that those who fear the Lord and speak often together about Him, are heard by the Lord "and a book of remembrance was written before him for them that feared the LORD, and that thought upon his name" (3:16).

13

Your Parents' Fault?

Psychiatrists often tell us that whatever is wrong with us is due to something our parents have done or have failed to do in bringing us up. Some teenagers find this judgment to be very convenient and satisfying. But psychiatrists do not intend to place the blame for your faults on your parents and stop there. The question is, "Where do you go from there?"

You do not want to wind up as many adults do, grown-up crybabies complaining that their parents' behavior twenty years ago is responsible for their present ills. One sure way to remain a crybaby is to continue to blame others.

In the first place, a Christian is enabled to forgive the mistakes other people make. No parent ever claimed to be perfect. Many parents see their mistakes and are genuinely sorry. Most parents do the best that they can under the human limitations imposed upon them. They are not psychologists and cannot be expected to know all the implications of their behavior.

Second, a Christian teenager must become responsible for his own conduct. He must correct his attitudes and habits if he wants to mature and cultivate his potentialities. A rule of thumb is "Make no excuses." Another good principle is "Face the facts."

The Lord will help any Christian who sincerely wants help. He understands us better than we or psychiatrists do.

Coping with life's problems is often exaggerated. True, some people underestimate difficulties, but most of us tend to exaggerate them. We take ourselves far too seriously.

To avoid too much self-occupation, make sure that every day you show interest in every member of your family, in your friends and group interests. Practice joy. Share gladness, good humor, surprise, and fun. In making other people happy you will find happiness.

"I am come that they might have life, and that they might have it more abundantly," Jesus said (Jn 10:10b). The Lord does not expect you to live a miserable, self-pitying existence; He wants your life to be rich and full of meaning, not only for yourself but for others. Open the doors and windows of your heart and let the sunshine of God's joy flood your soul. Let the fresh air of the Holy Spirit cleanse the cobwebs from your mind, and start living a fresh, vital life. Only Satan glories in your gloominess.

14

Standardized Tests

One high school boy counted thirty-three standardized tests that he had taken during twelve years of schooling! There are more than eighteen hundred such tests for math, English, science, social studies, and general intelligence testing. The average junior or senior takes about five such tests.

The purpose of testing is to predict a student's chance of success in college. As helpful as they are to this end, there are other factors not reflected by tests.

For instance, on an objective test such as multiple choice, true-false, or matching, a bright student may see many sides of the truth and see where a "right" answer is wrong to some degree. Also, the poor student can guess, and if he gets the right answer, it does not mean necessarily that he *knows* the right answer.

Furthermore, some students become very frightened when they take a test and cannot think clearly.

The greatest single factor that tests cannot determine is the desire on the part of the student to learn. Whereas one student may make all A's in high school, he may have all failures in college because his motives were different in each situation. A student who may do poorly in high school (because he has a temporary emotional problem) might perform brilliantly in college.

Your greatest asset in education is the burning desire to learn. God can use all the truth that you can master. Ask Him to create within you the motivation to learn. Study may be the hardest kind of work that you know, but it can be the means of glorifying God.

Do not be discouraged by low test scores. As valuable as they might be in evaluating your progress thus far, they do not determine the future. "Study to shew thyself approved unto God" (2 Ti 2:15a).

15

Modern Books

Christians in high school and college are sometimes confronted with the problem of being assigned reading matter that is not in keeping with Christian standards. Although realism can be presented in a wholesome manner, many modern authors believe that they must use vile language to be realistic.

Some persons in literary circles agree with this, but not all. A famous author, Paul Gallico, in his article, "Writers Should Be Heard But Not Obscene," has this to say about modern writing: "The wraps are off, everybody is a big boy now and allowed to write the dirty words, but the quality of the prose resulting from this freedom ought still to be confined to privy walls rather than published on clean, white paper manufactured at the sacrifice of honest trees. . . . If anything, writing seems to me to have become more juvenile and adolescent than ever I can remember."

We cheer this man who will speak out on what he feels to be right. Can we ask less of ourselves?

Literature, consciously or unconsciously, shapes our attitudes. Perhaps you are sure you would never use bad language; but if you constantly read it, the words become familiar and you become less sensitive to them. The Bible says that we are to be "wise in what is good, and innocent in what is evil". (**Ro** 16:19*b*, NASB).

Some young people explore the seamy side of life because of an unhealthy curiosity. The Bible says, "Do not participate in the unfruitful deeds of darkness, but instead even expose them; for it is disgraceful even to speak of the things which are done by them in secret" (Eph 5:11-12, NASB).

If you are assigned to read a filthy book, ask the Lord to enable you to refuse in a manner that will bring honor to His name. Speak privately with your instructor and do not incriminate him. Above all, observe the rules of Christian ethics, keeping this matter between yourself and the Lord, despite the cost to yourself. You may be ridiculed, you may fail the course, you may suffer other consequences, but you will have done the right thing.

Above all, do not use your Christian position to get out of doing your duty. Ask to be assigned another book, and do your very best work on the assignment. Thank your instructor for his consideration and show your appreciation.

There is too much that is beautiful and good in literature to settle for trash.

16

Good Sportsmanship

It's not easy to accept unfairness from umpires and referees. It's not easy to play your heart out and lose a game. It's not easy to not complain when you know the other team cheated its way to victory. It's not easy to congratulate the other team for winning. But all of this is "sportsmanship."

One of the greatest values of athletics is that it teaches the individual to be a good sport. Throughout life we are faced with unfair situations and disappointments. If we can accept them with a spirit of good sportsmanship we will reflect the teachings of our Lord who said, "I tell you, don't resist the man who wants to harm you. If a man hits your right cheek, turn the other to him as well" (Mt 5:39, Phillips).

Not all good sports are Christians and, unfortunately, not all Christians are good sports!

Thelma was a miserable girl until she finally made the girls' basketball team. The captain showed her special attention so that she gained self-confidence. She came to prize sportsmanship very highly and often spoke of it.

However, in the classroom she was not a good sport at all. If she did not like a certain teacher, she would

33

pout. If her grades weren't as high as she hoped they'd be, she blamed the teacher.

Could it be that Thelma was a good sport on the team only because she wanted the recognition of being a "good sport"?

If you are a good sport in one area of your life, let that characteristic carry over to the classroom and to your home. Resist the urge to get back at those who irritate you or to blame others for your own short-comings.

Maturity is taking responsibility for your own actions and keeping quiet about the wrongdoing of others.

17

You, the Leader

There is a lot of talk about what's wrong with young people, as if something were wrong with all of them. The truth is, there is still a majority who are decent. Granted that the majority is decent, everyone will agree that Christian young people are definitely in the minority.

Because they are few in number, some Christians blend in with the society in which they live and more or less conform to social patterns. If a Christian does not dance, smoke, drink, swear, etc., this goes somewhat unnoticed, for there are others who do not indulge in these things. The way you dress might mark you as different sooner than the fact that you don't tell dirty jokes.

Two librarians worked side by side for a whole year without either of them knowing that the other one was a Christian! What is wrong with a Christian who can live with the same people day in and day out and yet not reveal his identity as one of Christ's own?

It's the little matter of taking the initiative. This is the point where most of us fail. We do all the proper things and refrain from doing the improper, but our lives do not count for much unless we venture further.

You may not have natural leadership, but the reluctance of a Christian to set the standard, to set the pace, to start the conversation leaves the world without a challenge.

This does not mean that you must launch out in your own strength to let the world know what Christ has done for you, but it does mean that you subject yourself to the Holy Spirit and be willing to take whatever steps He directs. Instead of being on the defensive where the Lord is concerned, prepare yourself and take the offensive.

You may not know all the reasons for everything you believe in, but no one can effectively deny your own personal experience with the Lord. Your knowledge of the Bible and your own testimony might well alert another young person who callously brushes Him aside because he has never known anyone who took God seriously and believed that He works in life today.

Spiritual hunger is everywhere, but those who are the most hungry do not always realize what is wrong with them. Those who have sought answers have despaired of finding them. If a witness is to be given to young people it's up to you. The older generation is not nearly as effective.

18

The Value of Character

You may consider that you are too young to have much experience, but despite your youth, you probably have been in situations where you have witnessed the lack of character in people who should be persons of integrity. Perhaps you remember the first shock of seeing an adult deliberately lie or break the law. After a few such experiences, some youngsters get the idea that this is the only way to get ahead in the world of grownups.

However, our way of life cannot continue without the ethical and moral standards of Christianity. J. P. Morgan, outstanding Christian financier, was once asked if his credit was not based merely on the ability to put up property or other collateral for a loan. Mr. Morgan replied, "No, sir. The first thing is character."

"Before money or property?" the inquirer asked.

"Before money or anything else. Money cannot buy it. . . . Because a man I do not trust could not get money from me on all the bonds in Christendom," he replied.

How good is your character? When you make a promise, do you keep it? Can you take criticism? Can you work without being praised or rewarded? Are you truthful at all times? Are you dependable? Are you thrifty? Are you loyal?

Good character can be formed best as you yield yourself to the Lord Jesus Christ in positive effort to conform to the principles of God's Word. You are the only person who can damage your character or hinder its growth.

The word *character* comes from a Greek word which means a sharp-pointed instrument, such as an engraving tool. By character we make an impression on the world. Like a tool, character improves with use. It is to your advantage to forge a strong character and keep it in good condition.

There are many examples of men and women of character in the biographies of the truly great people in history. It took courage for William Jennings Bryan, a presidential candidate, to debate with Mr. Darrow on the issue of evolution. It took integrity for Theodore Roosevelt to rid Tammany Hall of its corruption. They risked their political futures and personal reputations, but both men went down in history as men of character.

19

Vices and Virtues

Someone smoking in President Lincoln's presence complimented him on having no vices for Lincoln did not smoke, drink, or swear.

"That is a doubtful compliment," Lincoln replied. "I recollect once being on a stage in Illinois when a man sitting by me offered me a cigar. I told him I had no vices. He said nothing, smoked for some time, and then grunted: 'It's my experience that folks who have no vices have few virtues.'"

Have you ever known a person who prided himself in the things he did not do but at the same time lacked anything of a positive nature in his life? A Christian must beware that he is not content with only refraining from doing that which he considers to be wrong. As Lincoln said on another occasion, "Some men seem to think that as long as they keep out of jail they have a sure chance of getting into heaven."

A person does not go to heaven by something he does do or by something he does not do. He goes to heaven by the grace of God. When a sinner accepts Christ he becomes a new creation; old things are passed away and all things become new, and all things are of God.

A hateful spirit is replaced by kindness and affection. A proud, boastful personality is replaced with humility and an unassuming manner. These changes may not take place overnight but they should be taking place continually as the Spirit reveals Himself to the believer.

A vacuum is a dangerous situation. Jesus told a parable about a man who was cleansed of a demon but his house was left empty. The evil spirit returned with seven more spirits to occupy the vacuum. If you have quit this or that bad habit, that is all well and good, but occupy your mind and heart with positive virtues and activities so that you will not become a sour, fruitless Christian. Take care that you do not pride yourself in what you do *not* do—or, for that matter, in what you do!

Paul wrote, "And be not conformed to this world"— but that is not the end of the statement—"but be ye transformed by the renewing of your mind, that ye may prove what is that good, and acceptable, and perfect, will of God" (Ro 12:2).

God has planned that every Christian will be "conformed to the image of his Son" (Ro 8:29).

To turn away from evil is very important, but it is equally important to undertake the doing of God's will.

20

Missionary Image

Unfortunately, missionaries do not always present the image that appeals to young people. When they return from a primitive country after five years abroad, they are not always on the wavelength of the American teenager. They have to catch up on a lot, and in the meantime they may appear to be a bit dull or outmoded.

Missionaries are not inclined toward self-exaltation; therefore, we aren't always aware of their heroic lives. The respect that such lives should demand is lost in the humility of the servant of Christ.

On the other hand, teenagers sometimes get the idea that missionaries are only martyrs, sacrificial, and deprived. They know themselves well enough to know that they could not stand up under sacrificial conditions and, although they admire the missionary, they discount the possibility of becoming missionaries themselves.

The truth is, the majority of the world's population is concentrated in cities. The picture of missionaries living in the jungle with savages, although not a thing of the past, is nevertheless being replaced by the vision of reaching the masses in the cities of the world.

Rapid communication and transportation, the increase in literacy around the world, and the modernization of living conditions give the missionary a more tolerable living situation than ever before. Scientific advancements have overcome many of the problems of language and social barriers.

The sacrifice of native land, family and friends, and the culture shock of adjusting to another environment remain, but many missionaries come to love their adopted country and its people so that our Lord's words are fulfilled: "Anyone who gives up his home, brothers, sisters, father, mother, children, or property, to follow Me, shall receive a hundred times as much in return" (Mt 19:29, Living NT).

21

The Call

One of the reasons young people don't volunteer for the mission field is because great emphasis is laid upon the fact that a Christian must be "called" to the field. If it is true that one must be called by God to be a missionary, isn't it also true that a Christian must be called to be a secretary or a banker or a professional person? Why such high spiritual demands upon the missionary when other careers are entered without much thought as to the will of God?

The fact is, many careers pursued in this country could be useful to the missionary enterprise abroad. Secretaries, bookstore clerks, doctors, pilots, radio technicians, musicians, mechanics, construction workers, teachers, etc., are desperately needed to further the gospel throughout the world. Preachers, evangelists, Christian education instructors, and Bible teachers are always in demand.

One might well approach the question of missionary service as he would consider any career in which he may be interested.

Inquire of various mission boards concerning the qualifications of candidates and the needs of the fields.

Confer with your pastor and other spiritual advisers.

Most of all, pray. If you are unwilling to go, ask the Lord to help you to truly surrender.

In this area you might examine your attitudes to see if you, like so many young people, have simply put the foreign field out of your mind as something absolutely not for you. The Lord may never have had your ear with regard to the field if you have closed your mind to it. Whatever the hindrance may be to your personal voluntary service overseas, you must face it honestly before you can have the assurance that any other form of work is His will for you. It is well to be willing to do the hardest job before we can be content doing the less difficult task.

22

Specific Guidance

We often hear or read messages about "how to know the will of God" and we often go to a lot of trouble to know God's will about specific decisions. But often we feel disappointed and think that we somehow missed the signals or did not wait or did not pray hard enough.

Has God promised to give specific guidance about everything in our lives? Remember the parable of the pounds? It is a story told by Jesus to illustrate our responsibility to God. A nobleman went away to receive a kingdom. Before he left he gave each of his servants a certain number of pounds with which to buy and trade. When he returned, he asked them to account for the money. The servant to whom he had given ten pounds had doubled the amount. The one who was given five had doubled his too. To each servant the nobleman gave authority over certain cities, commending them as faithful servants.

But the third servant, to whom one pound had been given, had done nothing to increase his Lord's investment. For him the nobleman had nothing but condemnation and said, "Take from him the pound, and give it to him that hath ten pounds" (Lk 19:24; see vv. 11-27).

This illustrates an important part of Christian living—the part played by initiative and industry. It is wrong to sit back and make no decision because specific guidance has not been given about a detail. God has provided principles by which Christians should operate. He has given Christians godly judgment through His Word, and He has a right to expect us to act on that judgment.

Do not be afraid that you will be leaning on your own wisdom if you sincerely submit yourself to the Lord and then proceed according to the best knowledge given you from the Word.

One day you will have to give an account for the time and ability which God has given you. If you have hesitated as did the disobedient servant because you were afraid of doing the wrong thing, you will be condemned even as he was. There is nothing pious or spiritual about doing nothing. It merely shows a lack of trust and obedience.

The Holy Spirit will give you confidence as you use the brain God has given you if you are sincere in your desire to glorify God. If you cannot accept the sphere of influence or authority committed to your trust now, you cannot expect to have greater authority given to you in the future when the King of kings returns.

23

Education

In an increasingly technical age, a young person must consider the importance of getting all the education that he can. Yet, what kind of education? As a Christian you would like to get training in a school that honors Christ; however, there are few accredited Christian colleges. To enter a profession you need a degree from an accredited college. Perhaps you cannot afford an extra year in a nonaccredited school.

Do these facts eliminate the possibility of a Christian education for you? They must not. As vital as education is, a Christian education is imperative. True, you may not complete your studies in a Christian institution, but you should spend as much time as possible in the study of God's Word. One year of intensive Bible study should precede university or other college work. If you are willing to put this first, the Lord will see you through the other necessary training.

Choose Bible courses that will help you withstand the attacks on Christian faith—courses such as "evidences" and "apologetics." Study of the Bible itself, history, exegesis, and analytical studies will furnish you with a background in God's Word to use in evangelism and in your devotional life.

No matter how anxious you may be to get your years of education behind you, give the Lord at least one year of intensive study. In a Christian school you can more thoroughly examine your commitment to Christ, investigate the possibilities of Christian work as your lifework, and settle your future.

You will be thinking of marriage within the next few years. It is more likely that you will meet Christian friends at a Christian school. You may be led to your life's partner.

Beware of making up your own mind about any college without consulting the Lord for His choice.

24

Choosing a Vocation

A Christian wants to know what God wants him to do with his life but sometimes he is confused about what God's will is for him. Sometimes he doesn't find out because he isn't truly willing to *do* God's will. The Lord reveals His will only to those who are willing to *do* His will.

How can you find the work God has for you? Sometimes the Lord reveals His will through answers to prayer, through the Word of God, and through circumstances. If you live in close fellowship with the Lord through Bible study and prayer, you will proceed in His will day by day. You will find His will in the path of duty. As you study in school and do the best that you can with the Lord's help in all areas of your life, you are fulfilling His will. As you proceed in the same obedient manner, you will be in God's will ten and twenty years from now.

You should take aptitude tests to find out where your natural abilities lie. But these tests only suggest what type work you are best suited for, and not all occupations or professions will be considered by those who read your tests. However, the tests can steer you away from work that you are totally unsuited for.

Having your heart set on a particular occupation does not necessarily mean that you would be happy in it.

At best, tests are imperfect. One Christian girl was told that, on the basis of her test, she would make an excellent bartender!

When you are young you sometimes rule out certain vocations as being out of the question for you. Jean made that mistake. She thought she would never want to be a teacher, but her parents asked her to take a course in practice teaching when she was in college. She did and found that she thoroughly enjoyed the work. Today she is a successful high school teacher. She found God's work in the path of duty. So will you.

25

Rejected

If you have not yet experienced rejection, sooner or later you will. Someone you love will choose someone else; you will fail to make the grade on a job that you particularly enjoy; you will be defeated in a student election. Some experiences of rejection can be devastating. A parent rejects a child, a community ostracizes an individual, a social group can exclude a person.

Since rejection of one kind or another is experienced by nearly every person, it is important to know how to meet it and how to extract all its value.

Our Lord Jesus Christ was rejected as no mere human being can be rejected: "He is despised and rejected of men; a man of sorrows, and acquainted with grief" (Is 53:3a). It is a comfort to know that the Lord understands how it feels to be rejected. Christ, the innocent one, suffered to such an extent that our suffering is inconsequential in comparison. Nevertheless, He cares about us.

Prayer will help you to overcome your disappointment so that you will not become bitter or vengeful. Respond graciously and kindly to those who have hurt you. Keep your feelings to yourself, but be sincere in acknowledging disappointment if asked.

A high school junior, who had worked hard for three years in the student government, was defeated in the presidential election by a candidate who had never served his school but was very popular. The defeated candidate pretended that he did not care by being overly friendly and seemingly happy. His pretense made it awkward for his friends, and his pride made his enemies gloat.

Suffering defeat can make us take stock to see why we were rejected. Was it overconfidence? Aggressiveness? Laziness? Carelessness? Indifference? Evil-speaking? Pride? Seek to correct the causes of your hurt and do not blame others.

Remember that a Christian always has acceptance with the Lord for he is "accepted in the Beloved." This should make fellowship with the Lord more precious to you than any human association. Your experience will make you more mindful of the needs of others who are rejected.

If you do not learn from your experience, you will repeat the lesson over and over. If you do not use the experience, your hurt will have been wasted.

Remember that ten years from now the anguish of this experience will have faded, but its effect will be for either good or evil in your life. Don't make any rash conclusions. Take time to let the Lord heal you.

26

Don't Blame the Lord!

Have you ever known a Christian who blamed his lack of popularity on the fact that he was a Christian? Sally was a fifteen-year-old who seemed to enjoy talking about how a young person must suffer as a Christian. The truth was she had never really suffered for Christ's sake at all! She was not well liked because she had a sharp tongue. All she ever did was criticize other young people who did not have Christian standards. They thought she felt that she was better than they were so they left her alone.

How could Sally expect an unconverted classmate to follow Christian standards? How could she condemn the sinner who had never heard the gospel? Sometimes she would "preach" to them, telling them they were going to hell and that they should not do the things they did, but she never *showed* them the love of the Lord Jesus Christ. The truth is, she didn't care very much that they were going to hell; she only wanted to make her point.

Perhaps you recognize some of the same traits within yourself. Do you have a feeling of responsibility and concern for those classmates whose actions annoy you? Do you care about winning them to Christ? Be honest. If you do not have a desire to help them, ask the Lord to make you concerned enough to make any sacrifice, and to give your time and energy to loving them to Christ.

"Love never faileth," the Bible says. Love always finds a way, and the love of Christ shed abroad in your heart will enable you to humbly seek the lost. You will then know that your goodness is not a credit to you but a gift of God.

Randy was a boy who went to church regularly and did all the things that were expected of him among Christians. In school he was an average student and stayed out of trouble, but he didn't take it upon himself to try to win anyone to Christ. People thought of him as a good guy, but they were not particularly impressed by the fact that he loved the Lord Jesus Christ. The fact is, he was satisfied with being saved and living what he called "a normal life."

Jesus spoke of hiding one's light under a bushel. A Christian does not have to be bad to do this; he can simply live unto himself. It may not be your nature to be friendly, but for Jesus' sake you should show kindness and interest toward everyone. You *are* your "brother's keeper," so what happens to him spiritually is partially your responsibility.

Cultivate one friend whom you believe needs Christ. Ask the Lord to give you opportunities to share Christ with him.

27

For Whom Christ Died

When a person is poor or downtrodden, it is easy to
feel sorry for him and to desire that he know the Lord
that he might have joy. But what about that hateful
teacher or employer? What about that cruel, selfish
neighbor? What about the wealthy hypocrite? How
easy it is to not be concerned for them because they
seem to deserve whatever ill may befall them—even
hell.

But Jesus died for every sinner, and He commands
that we witness to every creature. We cannot content
ourselves with caring for the down and out; we must
seek to win the lost who are personally distasteful to
us. Only the Holy Spirit can give love for the unlovely. There is no value in displaying false love.

One of the ways in which we are helped in loving
the unlovely is by trying to understand what makes a
person the way he is. As an old Indian proverb puts
it, you must walk in another man's moccasins before
you judge him. Reasons for hatefulness do not justify
a mean spirit, but knowing those reasons will make
you more tolerant.

Another help toward loving the unlovely is to look
for their good qualities. Try to think positively where
they are concerned.

Third, fulfill your responsibility in your relationship with them and you will lessen the conflicts. Don't justify yourself for wrong on the basis of their unreasonableness, etc. In fact, go the second mile toward pleasing them. "Love begets love," that is, when you love someone and show it, they often respond with love.

If you had known the rich young ruler, it is possible that you would have naturally despised him. (We tend to be jealous of those who seem to have life easy.) But, Jesus loved him. When the young man went away sorrowing because he could not part with his possessions, do you think Jesus stopped loving him? Hardly. He did not "mark him off his list," and neither should we mark off someone who does not come to the Lord when he has the opportunity.

If you will try to visualize what an individual will be like when he does become a Christian, this will build your faith and strengthen your love. As you pray for a person, your hostility toward him will lessen and God's love will seep in. You cannot, as a Christian, afford to let any resentment linger in your heart; for not only will it prevent you from loving the offending person, but bitterness will affect your own disposition and spiritual well-being.

Jesus loved even those who spit in His face and mocked Him. His love enabled Him to forgive them and to bear them no ill will. Hostility is of Satan and is one of his best weapons.

28

To Be Human

Have you ever noticed that when someone is trying to get acquainted with another person, one of the first questions he asks is, "What kind of work do you do?" This is part of getting to know someone. However, in some places people are considered to be important only according to how much they can do, or the kind of ability they have. And, some people judge others by what they have in the way of material possessions.

Immanuel Kant, the famous philosopher, stated, "Regard humanity in thyself and in others, always as an end and never as a mere means." He meant that a person is more than what he can do or what he has. More than that, a person is not to be "used" as a tool to gain something for you. Have you ever had a friend who always let you drive your car if you were going somewhere together, and also let you pay for the gas? Have you ever used a friend because he could influence someone in your behalf?

We are outraged when we hear of "influence peddling" in government, but if we use other people for our own advancement, we are guilty of the same violation of ethics.

Wouldn't you like to be always regarded as a human being rather than as a means to an end for someone else? Then that is the way we should regard all humanity. We are not to use people merely as a means to an end.

God made man in His own image. No higher dignity can be attributed to us. To regard a person or ourself as worthless because of lack of achievement or ability is to deny our basic humanity. Heaven, with all its glory, is the destiny of every Christian; therefore, it stands to reason that we are important to God. Even the fact of hell testifies to the uniqueness of man. You have never heard anyone even jokingly speak of a dog going to hell. Only man has been given the supreme dignity of a moral nature to be judged good or evil. Therefore, regard every man as a being made in the image of God. That image may be gravely spoiled but the ruins are there; and through the power of Christ's shed blood, that image can be restored.

God loved man enough to send His only Son to die for him. He does not ask, "Where do you work? Where do you live? How much do you have?" There is no such respect for persons with God, for He regards all men to be spiritually needy, and He loves all men equally.

Resolve never to use another person for your own advantage. Ask God to help you regard all men with compassion and concern.

29

Life After Death

When you go to college you will probably study the different philosophers and you will find that each of them has a theory about what takes place after death. Many philosophies as well as religions teach that there is no life after death.

Some students will follow Plato, others Descartes, Bultmann, or Russell. The Christian follows the Lord Jesus Christ who spoke a great deal about life after death. In fact, He spoke more about hell than He did heaven.

From the Scriptures we learn that man is actually more alive after death than he was when he was alive physically. In the story of the rich man and Lazarus (Lk 16:19-31), we are given a glimpse of man's condition after death. The rich man was in torment; Lazarus in peace. Both men were conscious and knew what was going on. There was no second chance after death for the rich man.

The Bible teaches us that "now we see through a glass, darkly," that is, we don't understand everything there is to know, "but then face to face: now I know in part; but then shall I know even as also I am known" (1 Co 13:12). As the Lord knows us (every hair of our heads!) even so we shall know all that He wants us to know.

The eternal state is not to be thought of as something far away. Eternal beings have been revealed at the very "elbows" of God's people. Take the case of Elisha when threatened by the Syrian soldiers surrounding Dothan: Elisha was unafraid because he knew that the angels stood between him and his enemy. Elisha asked the Lord to reveal the angels to his servant and it was done. "And the LORD opened the eyes of the young man; and he saw: and, behold, the mountain was full of horses and chariots of fire round about Elisha" (2 Ki 6:17).

The Bible tells us that "the angel of the LORD encampeth round about them that fear him, and delivereth them" (Ps 34:7). We are told that where two or three are gathered together in Jesus' name, there He is in their midst (Mt 18:20).

The eternal state could be revealed instantly to us if God so desired. Some men have caught a glimpse through visions and dreams. Paul was "caught up to the third heaven" (2 Co 12:2-4). "And he heard utterances beyond the power of man to put into words, which man is not permitted to utter" (v. 4, Amplified).

John saw heaven and recorded most of what he saw in the Revelation. Heaven is as near to us as it was to Paul and to John.

30

Sharing

God has His own mathematics. When Jesus shared the five loaves and two fishes, they multiplied. When we share our scant possessions, He multiplies them. As the lunch was divided, it increased! The same paradox is apparent with us, for when we give we receive! "Give, and it shall be given.unto you; good measure, pressed down, and . . . running over" (Lk 6:38). The reverse is also true: "He which soweth sparingly shall reap also sparingly" (2 Co 9:6a).

Sometimes we look at the pitifully small amount of money that we have to give, but we should look at what God can do with the smallest amount. He took the two mites of the widow, and her story has brought untold blessing to millions of people.

Money is not the principal thing we have to give. When Peter and John went up the temple stairs they had no money to give to the lame man who begged, but they gave him something money could not buy. Peter said, "Silver and gold have I none; but such as I have give I thee: In the name of Jesus Christ of Nazareth rise up and walk" (Ac 3:6).

You may not have money or the gift of healing, but you, like Peter, can say, "I will give you what I have," and that might be much more important than money.

You have love, joy, peace, and helping friendship to offer in Christ's name. In turn, you will receive the special joy that comes with giving, for, indeed, "It is more blessed to give than to receive" (Ac 20:35*b*).

We can never outgive God. It is as if we ladled out our gifts with a sugar spoon, whereas He shovels out our blessings with a snow shovel! "Freely ye have received, freely give" (Mt 10:8*b*).

David understood the truth, "We give thee but thine own," for he said, "But who am I, and what is my people, that we should be able to offer so willingly after this sort? For all things come of thee, and of thine own have we given thee" (1 Ch 29:14). Our talents, our abilities, our opportunities, and our strength are all gifts from God, so in spending them for Him we are giving Him but His own.

The Bible says that "God loveth a cheerful giver" (2 Co 9:7*b*), and we may rest assured that a cheerful giver loves God!

In fact, if giving is burdensome, or if you give "out of necessity," it would be just as well for you not to give. The cattle on a thousand hills belong to God, and if He needed anything He would certainly not ask us or any man.

Giving is a privilege to delight the soul of the giver. Perhaps you find it bothersome to give your time to activities concerning Christianity or to give your friendship to someone who needs you. Ask the Lord to give you a willing heart and a right attitude.

31

Optimism

To be an optimist means that one always looks on the bright side of things. Is there any biblical basis for being an optimist? There seems to be a very sound basis in Scripture. "Now abide faith, hope, love" (1 Co 13:13, NASB). *Hope* is another word for optimism. Here we find hope listed among the three greatest virtues.

Gloomy Christians certainly are not hopeful, are they? They may be honest, loving, and kind, but they probably don't expect results! The Bible tells the Christian that he should "plow in hope" (1 Co 9:10), that is, look for a harvest.

The Bible also says that hope comes as the result of trial. During trials or difficulties the Christian develops patience, and after patience, hope. Patience gives us experience so that we realize that we will get through life even though it is evil or a struggle. That produces hope.

"Suffering produces endurance, and endurance, tested character, and tested character, hope" (Ro 5:3*b*-4, NASB).

A pessimist (the opposite of an optimist), can never appreciate the second coming of Christ, which is called the "blessed hope." He cannot understand why God permits evil. If he had his ideal world we would all be holy and have no troubles at all.

The optimistic Christian knows that evil is the natural result when man follows his own way instead of God's. But he realizes that we would be mere puppets if God stopped evil and forced everyone to obey Him. He also is aware that God has promised to use evil in a constructive way in the Christian's life, for through trials the Christian proves God's strength and power. He also experiences God's loving forgiveness and is made aware of His holiness.

Hope will make every day brighter and lift every burden so that it is lighter than before. Hope is very useful to a radiant Christian life.

When we reach heaven, our fondest hopes will be more than realized. We shall never be ashamed or disappointed because we hoped in God. "Eye hath not seen, nor ear heard, neither have entered into the heart of man, the things which God hath prepared for them that love him" (1 Co 2:9).

We are told to "hope to the end" (1 Pe 1:13). God would not mock us and command us to be hopeful when there is nothing to hope for. Of course we are not to pin our hopes on anything or anyone but upon Him. "Hope thou in God" (Ps 43:5; 42:5, 11).

Hope is not idle wishing but a genuine trust in God. It is trust based on His goodness and ability. Pin your hope upon Him and you will not be disappointed. To despair is to deny God's goodness and to cheat oneself of the joy of believing. Only unbelievers are to be without hope (Eph 2:12; 1 Th 4:13).

32

Tempting God

Do you ever take your life in your own hands? Do you ever ride in an automobile with a driver who speeds?

A sixth-grade boy came to school boasting of having ridden in a high-powered automobile at a fast rate of speed. His teacher knew the man who drove the car and the thought flashed through her mind that the boy would one day be old enough to be behind a steering wheel and that he would quite likely drive too fast— just like the man he admired.

Five years later, that boy and another person were killed in a speeding automobile. Both victims had professed faith in the Lord Jesus Christ, but they were being careless with their lives. When we deliberately take chances with our lives, we are tempting God to take them. When Satan suggested to Jesus that He jump down from the pinnacle of the temple, he quoted the psalm about angels taking charge of Him so that He would not cut His foot on a stone.

The devil was misusing Scripture by saying that nothing could happen to one who belongs to God. Young people often have the notion that nothing can happen to them until their time comes. They, too, are mistaken.

Jesus did not jump down from the pinnacle. He told Satan, "As it is written, Thou shalt not tempt the Lord thy God."

We can tempt God in other ways. If we deliberately play around with sin, we have no guarantee of God's protection. A girl who insists upon going with a boy who is not a Christian, may fall in love with him. If her life is not ruined through marriage to him, her heart may be broken by breaking off the relationship.

We can tempt God by indifference. Do you not fear for our nation when you observe how marvelously she has been spared from enemy attack and has been blessed, and yet, many Americans don't give the Lord a second thought? Do you not fear that the judgment of God will fall upon her?

Likewise, an individual Christian needs to beware of indifference and carelessness in his attitude toward the Lord. God may find it necessary to chastise the believer with trials and tribulation if he does not respond to all the Lord's goodness.

No child of God can claim a "charmed life" simply because he believes in the Lord Jesus Christ. Nevertheless, it is a serious thing to tempt God by flaunting willfulness and carelessness in His face. Keep your heart with all diligence toward the Lord.

33

Vanity

In California a hairdresser set up a booth at a fair to demonstrate hairstyling, and most of the customers were boys! One boy had his hair dyed blue.

In the art world, monkeys are employed to smear paint on canvas, and their "paintings" bring high prices in competition with human artists' abstract paintings.

In John Bunyan's classic, *Pilgrim's Progress*, a place called "Vanity Fair" is described. In Christian's journey he encountered all the vainglorious attractions of Vanity Fair.

So do you! The world has always had its foolish vanities and always will. In the rapid change of fads it takes an expert to keep up with fashions of this world (providing that he cares to do so).

Bizzare styles of dress express the self-image a person wants to project. If he wants to appear as a fool, he does so. Neurotic tendencies are clearly displayed.

There is no virtue in being unattractive or drab, but a Christian should express his character in the way he dresses. An integrated personality shows itself in carefully chosen clothing. There is no excuse for sloppiness or disorderliness. Polished shoes, clean, brushed hair, pretty colors, and modest fittings combine to give a witness. Clothes do not make the man, but clothes are expressive of what kind of person you are. The vanities that you may pass up will never be missed. Rather, your friends will sense your stability and strength of character in being yourself, not a clown.

There are many vanities besides those of dress. Time and money spent on that which is worthless is vanity. There is also the vanity of one's own person. Sir Max Beerbohm once said, "To say that a man is vain means merely that he is pleased with the effect he produces on other people. A conceited man is satisfied with the effect he produces on himself."

There is the vanity of accomplishment, whether on the football field or in the classroom. Solomon, in despair, wrote, "Vanity of vanities, saith the Preacher, vanity of vanities; all is vanity" (Ecc 1:2). Well, it need not be! The difference is simple—are we what we are and do we do what we do for the glory of God or for the glory of self?

34

Getting Even

Have you ever watched the way some grownups act when they encounter an unpleasant person? For example, the fellow at the service station—he couldn't care less how he serves the customers. Your Uncle Charlie, who is ordinarily a nice man, drives up to the pump and waits for Jake to come out and fill up the tank. Finally he beeps the horn. Even then, Jake takes his own good time to appear. He doesn't return Uncle Charlie's greeting, he just grunts.

Jake takes the cap off the gas tank and then stands talking to a friend. Uncle Charlie is getting impatient, so he leans his head out the window and yells, "Don't fill it too full." Then he explains to you that when it's too full it is wasted because hot weather makes the gas expand and spill over. By the time he finishes the explanation, you hear the gas that has been pouring into the tank now spilling onto the concrete. Jake is so interested in what his friend is saying he doesn't notice.

"Uncle Charlie, I think it's spilling over," you say quietly.

"Hey!" your uncle yells, jumping out of the car.

Jake nonchalantly withdraws the nozzle and hooks it onto the tank. Uncle Charlie is furious. Jake shrugs his shoulders. "What's so terrible about a couple drops of gas?"

Uncle Charlie slams the money into Jake's hand, jumps into the car and jerks it into gear. He is fighting mad!

Uncle Charlie reacted with anger toward Jake. Even though he did not admire the shiftless man, he behaved in a manner that was no better than Jake's. He lost his temper and accomplished nothing. He had acted childishly.

Don't let people trap you into reacting badly, into trying to get even. The Bible says, "Be not overcome of evil, but overcome evil with good" (Ro 12:21).

Life is filled with irritations, annoyances, and aggravations. If it isn't some *one* it is some *thing*. But a Christian has the ability to adjust to a situation because God has promised him the grace to overcome. A spiritually mature person can overlook a grievance without becoming upset. A "meek and quiet spirit" is not weakness; it is true strength. It is endurance.

A self-centered person reacts quickly when he thinks his rights have been ignored. But a Christ-centered person looks for opportunities to demonstrate the grace of our Lord Jesus Christ. He is more interested in winning others to the Lord than in defending himself.

35

No Temptation?

With all the publicity about the physical harm done by smoking, one would think it would be comparatively easy for a young person to refrain from acquiring the habit. In some situations this may be true. Living among your family and Christian friends you probably don't feel that you would ever even want to smoke. However, your present situation is not permanent. Someday you may be thrust into a situation where smoking will be a real temptation. In the company of so-called sophisticated people, persons that you, admittedly, want to impress, you may take that first cigarette.

Because drinking alcohol is even more dangerous, you may feel that you will never be tempted to drink. Experience may well prove that you will be more strongly tempted to take a drink than to smoke. In society you may well be made to feel that you are spurning a hostess' hospitality. You may be ridiculed or harrassed into taking a drink.

For example, perhaps you will be in the armed services and receive a promotion. Customarily a serviceman has a party to celebrate. Other men serve champagne, a costly drink. If you do not, they may think that you are not willing to spend the money.

71

Even if you don't drink, they don't enjoy a party without alcohol.

Or, maybe you will be invited to an engagement party. Not to sip the toast might offend the honoree.

You will be tempted by the intellectual arguments—persuasion based on the assumption that you need to get away from your narrow upbringing and find things out for yourself.

Remember this verse for such occasions: "No temptation has come your way that is too hard for flesh and blood to bear. But God can be trusted not to allow you to suffer any temptation beyond your powers of endurance. He will see to it that every temptation has a way out, so that it will never be impossible for you to bear it" (1 Co 10:13, Phillips).

36

From Bad to Worse

Her home was unpleasant; she had many responsibilities. When her boyfriend felt sorry for her and
asked her to marry him, she did. She thought she
would escape unpleasantness and find happiness. The
young couple did not have enough money to provide
for their necessities. A child came, and matters became unbearable.

A boy with similar circumstances decided to join the
service to get away from it all. For a while it seemed
like a wise thing to do, but as he grew older he realized
what he had missed by dropping out of school. He
was faced with temptations that he was too young to
resist. He blamed his parents for letting him join the
service.

"From bad to worse" can become a pattern of life.
Some adults finally take their own lives because they
think nothing could be worse than their circumstances.
How dreadful to think that problems can be solved
by running away from them.

What does it mean to resist the urge to run away?
It means to face the facts. When we survey a situation
it is well to remember that no matter how good or how
bad circumstances may be, they will change. You can

ride out any storm because storms do not last forever. Consider how long you have been able to endure, and you will be strengthened to know that you can withstand a bit longer. The Bible says, "My grace is enough for you: for where there is weakness, my power is shown the more completely" (2 Co 12:9*a*, Phillips).

There are also ways to "escape" which don't include running away (see 1 Co 10:13). You can improve your situation by the right attitude, by prayer, and by exercising greater love. You may also find release in talking with a Christian who will keep your confidence. If you go through difficulties rather than running away, you will grow strong.

37

Teenage Conformity?

A Christian boy complained that this is an age of conformity and that since a Christian can't go along with all that unbelievers do, he is considered "square" and "out of it."

Undoubtedly there is truth in his observation, but isn't it also true that this is an age of *non*conformity? Young people are doing all kinds of strange things to throw off conformity. If their nonconformity is real, then they will appreciate the Christian who is a nonconformist.

Granted that some young people will try to discourage a Christian in every way that they can, it is also true that if a Christian is the kind of person our Lord died to make him, he will have an irresistible appeal. The kindness, generosity, gentleness, helpfulness, honesty, and love that pour from a Christian heart form a fountain of goodness to which nearly everyone is attracted.

Sometimes Christians hear so much about being scorned that they come to expect it. In defense, they sometimes withdraw into their circle of Christian friends. The Lord, on the other hand, ate with "publicans and harlots," sinners of all kinds. Undoubtedly they found Him attractive even if they disagreed with Him.

Witnessing for Christ has never been easy, for Satan sets up every roadblock that he can to prevent it. The most effective roadblocks are the Christian himself and the preconceived ideas which he has about how his witness will be received. The young Christian mentioned in the beginning should also realize that not all conformists are happy in their conformity. Christians whose witness is rejected are often personally rejected because they do not live a life that measures up to the godliness that Jesus died to give. When others truly see Christ in us, they will desire Him and want what we have, and soon, talking about the Lord will be as natural as talking about anyone else.

38

Fitness

Within the last decade Americans have become aware of the need for physical fitness. So many young men were turned down for military service because of physical unfitness that the government instituted programs to correct the problem. Now schools put a stronger emphasis on physical exercise and health education. Adults swarm to health clubs, gymnasiums, and recreational facilities to improve their physical well-being. Exercise programs on television are popular with housewives.

When the Russians sent up their first sputnik, Americans became alarmed about our educational system. Schools immediately felt the effects, and students have become more mentally fit through educational reforms.

What about "spiritual fitness"? Of course, one cannot expect unbelievers to be "spiritually fit," but what about Christians? Are we fit for the competition we face?

In much the same way that a person gets in good physical or mental shape, he can get in good spiritual condition. He begins to follow a regular program of study and exercise. The Bible says, "Work hard so God can say to you, 'Well done.' Be a good workman, one who does not need to be ashamed when God examines your work. Know what His Word says and means" (2 Ti 2:15, Living NT); and "spend your time and energy in the exercise of keeping spiritually fit" (1 Ti 4:7*b*, Living NT).

The phrase from 1 Timothy 4:7*b* means to put into practice whatever you know to be godly. "Bodily exercise is all right, but spiritual exercise is much more important and is a tonic for all you do" (1 Ti 4:8*a*, Living NT). Compared to the values of exercising in a spiritual way, exercising physically is of little profit.

Your spiritual fitness as a member of the rising generation will determine the spiritual strength of the nation and the world. Seek out a mature Christian who can help you to grow strong through a concentrated effort.

39

Understanding

If there is any one complaint from teenagers that is heard more than others, it is that no one understands them. Without arguing the point, is it possible that teenagers understand adults? Isn't it true that high school students make general statements about all parents? They say that adults do not listen—they do not care—they only nag. Are these things *always* true?

A wise woman was asked how a bride might be sure of keeping her marriage happy. She said, "Never say *always*." What she meant is that no one *always* behaves in the same way. A husband may track mud on the floor sometimes but never always. Parents may not understand their children sometimes, but not always.

What effort do you make to understand your parents' point of view? Is it possible that you misunderstand them? Do you ever consider their sacrifices, their needs, their problems? Do you know what makes them feel the way they do and act the way they do? Have you no compassion for them?

Won't you admit that they *could* be right when you disagree with them? Isn't it possible that their experience and age enable them to know much more than you do about life? Isn't it logical that they would know better what is good for you than you do?

The Bible says, "Who can understand his errors?" (Ps 19:12a). "How can a man . . . understand his own way?" (Pr 20:24b). That means that we cannot clearly understand ourselves—we usually put ourselves in the best light and others in the worst light. Prayer will help you to understand yourself as well as others. As you begin to understand your parents, conflicts will be eased and tensions lessened.

40

Maturity

Many young people are far advanced in their psychological maturity, and there are adults who have never "grown up" psychologically.

Sometimes adults try to shame teenagers for not being "mature" when the truth is that teenagers are not supposed to be mature.

Maturity means accepting responsibility. There are various kinds of responsibility. Some girls have had household responsibilities since they were young children. Some boys have had the responsibility for younger children since they were quite young. Others have had jobs outside the home. However, work responsibility is not the only kind of responsibility—although perhaps it is the easiest kind to accept. There is the responsibility of making decisions, of working independently, assuming initiative. When a person acts responsibly, he is mature. When he acts irresponsibly, he is immature.

How mature are you in your spiritual life? Are you dependent upon others to supply your spiritual needs—Sunday school and church, Christian friends and parents? The mature Christian may take advantage of all these aids to spiritual growth, but he assumes the responsibility for his own growth by personal fellowship with the Lord.

Great Christians have been devoted to the personal study of the Bible and to private prayer. As a young Christian, no one expects you to be spiritually mature. Most Christians your age are still feeding on the "milk" of the Word, still unable to understand the deeper teachings of the Bible. But, as many of you show greater psychological maturity than some adults, it is also possible that you can become more spiritually mature than your elders. The majority of great Christians began to study God's Word at an early age and to employ obedient hearts to the Bible.

41

Loneliness

Some of the loneliest people in the world are Christians—especially young people. A nice girl may find herself sitting at home more often than the girl with no principles. The boy who participates in athletics may find himself very much alone in the midst of his teammates when the talk reeks with profanity and dirty jokes. As you grow older you will find other social and business situations in which you will feel alone.

A teacher who is a Christian found that she had very little in common with her fellow teachers when they went to a convention in a distant city. The nonchristian teachers went to amusements that the Christian did not want to attend. There were parties that involved drinking. But one morning the same group got up early to go horseback riding. The Christian was very sorry that she had not learned to ride when she was young. "There I was, declining nearly every invitation because of Christian principles," she said, "and along comes a perfectly legitimate recreation, and I had to decline that one, too. My colleagues must have felt exasperated with trying to include me."

It is well to cultivate interests, hobbies, and pastimes that are wholesome when you are young so that your

Christianity does not give non-Christians the idea that you are negative to all enjoyment.

The Lord understands our need for human companionship. Even though we may not participate in the evil of the world, we are nevertheless sent forth to mingle with the mainstream of humanity. We should do whatever we can to free ourselves from the isolation that segregates many Christians.

42

Nobody to Listen

A high school teacher was struck by the fact that most of her students had very little interest in going home after classes were over. She asked why.

"There's nobody at home, but if they were there there would be nothing but quarreling," one student replied.

"Tell me," asked the teacher, "if I were your mother, what could I do to be a good mother to you?"

Without hesitation, the class responded. "Just *listen* to us!"

Perhaps you feel the way those city students felt—that there is never anyone to listen to you. Usually there is someone to lecture or scold, but no one who will hear you out.

That is a very discouraging situation. You feel that you are entitled to more consideration than you get because you are young. However, you will find that life is full of discouraging situations. And one of the most discouraging is not having anyone who will simply listen to us.

There are two values in not being listened to. First, you will more readily appreciate God's listening, and second, you will appreciate other people's need to be heard. You will be able to say with the psalmist, "I love the LORD, because he hath heard my voice" (Ps 116:1).

If the Lord listens to you, don't you think that you should listen to Him? With Samuel, you should say, "Speak; for thy servant heareth" (1 Sa 3:10*b*).

To listen to other people who want to talk out their problems can be a means of relieving them. To air a troublesome situation sometimes reveals the solution. Sometimes in the telling the emotional intensity is released. By repeating the unpleasantness, its importance fades, and the person can go on to other things.

When it involves hearing the other person's viewpoint in a situation where you are involved (such as hearing your parents' side of the story), you will gain understanding.

Always you can direct those to whom you listen to the Lord whose "ear" is not "heavy" (or deaf) "that it cannot hear" (Is 59:1*b*).

43

What's Your Problem?

When asked what his problem was, an eighteen-year-old high school boy answered, "People run me down. My friends don't seem to care too much for me. Teachers can't understand me. I can't get anywhere with girls. I'm too self-critical. I'm too shy around girls. I'm a weak person."

This boy's family is poor. His father feeds pigs for a living. The boy finds escape in playing pool most of the night, therefore he is sleepy in school. It doesn't take a psychologist to understand a few things about him. You can tell that he has a very low opinion of himself. What would you do as a fellow classmate to help him?

Whatever you would do, the chances are that if you look hard enough in your own school you will find a boy or girl similar to this boy.

Most people leave this boy alone and truly do not care that he is so needy. They don't want to get personally involved.

Think of your own problems. They are probably less than this boy's, yet, do you not feel that you have a right to be heard and helped? Would you care to be brushed aside with the excuse, "That's his tough luck," or "There's nothing I can do"?

Somehow respectable people expect favors, and those who are unrespectable are not given a second thought.

Jesus said that we are to care for "the least of these my brethren." The unattractive outcast is the kind we think least of. We are willing to help a friend. Sometimes we help the outcast with our money, but not with personal friendship.

This boy needs to feel accepted, and only people his own age can make him feel that he belongs. How very much a Christian boy could do for him! With encouragement, suggestion, companionship, and fun, this boy would blossom. How great is the opportunity to win him to the Lord that he might find acceptance "in the Beloved."

How much a young people's group could do for this fellow by taking him into their circle, by including him in every way. Sometimes Christian young people are the most exclusive group in town because they are content with being with each other. They selfishly enjoy their fellowship and do not concern themselves about the needs of outsiders.

In your own community there are people your own age who feel that the world does not care whether they live or die. Only a young person knows how to help another young person who feels this way. Only you know how to make them feel at ease without making them sense that you are giving charity. Adults cannot assume this responsibility that you have with regard to your own age group. That lonely person is no farther from you than your telephone right now.

44

Advice for Problems

Every day Grace waited for the teacher. She wanted to talk about her problems. The teacher would take most of her lunch hour or an hour or so after school to listen to Grace's woes. Then she would offer definite suggestions to the girl, but Grace would only shrug her shoulders, and the next day she would be back again.

Sometimes she wouldn't say anything definite but would talk about "the way things have piled up" or say that "something's got to give." She talked about vague situations and ideas but never told the teacher that her father was an alcoholic and that her sister was beautiful and she wasn't. These were her real problems—the others were imaginary.

When one teacher felt that she had done all that she could to help Grace, the girl would find another teacher to haunt.

What was the matter with Grace? Apparently she wasn't truly interested in solving her problems. Perhaps she wanted attention. Undoubtedly she was unhappy, even miserable, but she might have enjoyed being miserable.

Grace is her own worst enemy. As she revolves around herself—always brooding over problems real or imaginary—she loses out on friendships and normal satisfactions. Although she is a very needy girl, she has set up defenses to keep anyone from getting through to her.

If you find yourself always seeking counsel but never acting upon it, be honest. Ask yourself why. Is it fair to continue taking up the time of those from whom you ask help if you don't intend to act on their advice and do something to help yourself? Do not hide behind the excuse that it helps you to let off steam. As true as that may be—and most counselors are very patient because they know it is a relief to tell someone our troubles—nevertheless, you cannot continue to simply talk indefinitely if more can be done. Play the game fairly. If you ask someone to listen, be courteous enough to listen to him when he tries to help you.

When our world revolves only around ourselves and we think too much about our personal problems, we become very dull company to others. The Bible says, "None of you should think only of his own affairs, but each should learn to see things from other people's point of view" (Phil 2:4, Phillips).

It is quite all right to talk to advisers about our problems, but we are to bear the responsibility that is ours in solving them. Paul said, "For every man shall bear his own burden" (Gal 6:5). In the final analysis we must each work out the solutions to our own problems.

45

Amber

Amber is the oldest gem known to mankind. Perhaps you have seen this glasslike substance, smooth to the touch, very light in weight, beautiful in colors varying from water-white to black. The most popular ambers are clear golden yellow, cloudy buttercup yellow, or opaque and antique brown.

Amber and the diamond are the only gems of vegetable origin. Some scientists say that the frigid Baltic Sea was as warm as the southern Mediterranean of today. Giant conifers, larger than our redwoods, grew in luxurious splendor on its shores. Then came the glacial ages and other changes which left these trees in a state of petrification.

The golden sap of these ancient trees hardened under the pressures and became the prized stone we call amber. The sap trapped small bits of vegetation, insect life, and even tiny drops of water. By cutting off the air, amber has held the particles in a perfect state of preservation. The bits of matter made the gem lovely, and time has made it valuable.

Time is precious to us who have an average life-span of seventy years. But to the Lord, who is "from everlasting to everlasting," three billion years may be spent forming a beautiful gem to delight His creatures.

Amber has been called "the gem of the ages" but God is the "Ancient of Days."

When we are young we are sometimes eager to get things done; or, we may have the attitude, "I have plenty of time." Neither viewpoint is necessarily true. Every activity has its own time, it's own importance. We need God's perspective.

Of Him it has been revealed that "One day is with the Lord as a thousand years, and a thousand years as one day" (2 Pe 3:8*b*).

46

A Time to Rest

In the race against time, many people have forgotten the importance of resting. Even Christians sometimes feel guilty if they are not busy.

Our Lord believed in rest periods and vacations. He told His disciples to "come apart and rest a while." They got into a ship and crossed the Sea of Galilee to a less-populated area. Our Lord Himself sometimes left the crowd when they were pressing in upon Him with their needs.

It is sometimes difficult to know where to draw the line. If you are a talented person, you are sometimes asked to do things because you do them well. However, the individual who asks you might profit by having to do the task himself. You cannot follow the rule of "never say no" because you may be going against the Lord's will by saying yes.

Isn't it reasonable to set a certain amount of time aside for sleeping—as much as you think you need? The trouble with some teenagers is that they sit up late and want to sleep all day.

Second, you need time to be alone. The Christian's mind often reverts to the Lord when he is quiet. While "alone with God" he can run over in his mind the things he wants to share with the Lord.

Earning the rest will make it all the more a treat. As you slave away at some disagreeable chore, you can look forward to that time set aside for relaxation.

Elijah gave in to despondency one time, all because he was physically worn out. He had run from Mount Carmel to the city of Jezreel. When he arrived in the city he learned that Jezebel, the wicked queen, had sworn to kill him by the next night. Elijah immediately left town and traveled all the way to Beer-sheba, the last town before the desert of Sinai. Then he went a day's journey into the desert.

He seemed almost aimless in his destination. An angel of the Lord found him under a juniper bush and asked him what he was doing there. Elijah complained that he had served faithfully but that everyone else had turned away from the Lord. He wished that he would die! The angel did not argue with Elijah. Instead, the angel gave him food to eat. After Elijah ate, he fell asleep.

Again the angel came to him and asked him the same question. Elijah repeated his answer and again the angel fed him.

God knew that the lack of rest and food was the cause of Elijah's depression. That is why he fed Elijah and let him sleep. All the "spiritual exercises" (praying, Bible reading, etc.) would not do what physical rest would do when he was exhausted.

Don't make the mistake of burning the candle at both ends so that depression and fatigue set in. Allow time for mental and physical rest. Jesus did!

47

Literally?

A young woman asked a teacher when she should take the Bible literally and when she should interpret it another way.

She had been influenced by modern teachers who say that the Bible is not the inspired Word of God. They teach that the Bible is the Word of God only when it speaks to an individual's heart.

If the Bible is God's Word only when it speaks to my heart, then my mind, not God's Word, is the ruling authority in life. God makes clear that His Word is the only infallible authority.

They say that the Bible must be "demythologized," which means that Scripture does not mean exactly what it says but has a hidden meaning.

Modern teachers ridicule the idea of the inspiration of the Scriptures by saying we take the Bible "literally." This is a misnomer because it implies that a conservative Christian does not know the difference between literal and figurative language and that he does not recognize idiomatic speech when he reads it!

If we took every word literally, we would believe the earth is square, because Scripture speaks of the "four corners of the earth." That would be ridiculous!

The Bible should be read as God's inspired Word,

full of authority and meaning. But it also should be read as all literature is read, with the attitude that the writing will have figurative expressions, parables, allegories, poetry, and prose. A good rule to follow is, if the first sense makes sense, accept it. That is, if a verse can be accepted literally, take it literally. If not, *then* compare it with other Scriptures for the meaning.

Scripture is meant to be read by common men with limited education and intelligence as well as by scholars. God did not prepare a Bible to mean two different things—one for the ignorant and one for the intellectual. God's Word is for all people in all circumstances, and it is plain enough so that any ordinary person can understand.

48

Curiosity

A healthy curiosity is a valuable asset. How inquisitive are you? Have you ever wondered where the expression "OK" comes from?

When President Martin Van Buren was in the White House, a depression had struck the country, causing great poverty. Although the President took measures to stop the depression, he personally spent a great deal of money on his estate called "Old Kinderhook."

In the next election, the Democrats made this lavish spending a campaign issue. "OK" became a slang expression for anything that was all right since it stood for "Old Kinderhook," which Van Buren justified as legitimate spending. Today, "OK" applies to anything approved.

You may not be curious about language but are fascinated by such things as engines or the personal lives of famous people. Everyone has a certain amount of inquisitiveness. It is well to cultivate a healthy curiosity.

Unfortunately, some people use curiosity in a wrong way. A gossip spends time minding other people's business. The evil-minded person searches for filth. The Bible teaches, "I want to see you experts in good, and not even beginners in evil" (Ro 16:9, Phillips).

Apply your curiosity to the Word of God. For example, what does the Bible teach about death? This subject remains a mystery to many learned men because they do not take the Bible seriously. What does the Bible say about the future of history? What does the Bible say about heaven? What does the Bible reveal about angels?

The Bible is the only source for many interesting subjects of thought. Moreover, the Bible can be depended upon as no history or science book can be depended upon because it is God's Word.

Every day you can add to your knowledge, for the Scripture must be learned "precept upon precept, line upon line." Or, little by little.

There are helps to Bible study. Bible institutes offer correspondence courses in different books of the Bible or according to certain subjects. Christian bookstores offer a good selection of Bible study books. Your pastor can direct you in your choices.

But, learning the Bible is something that cannot be done for you by someone else. You must have a keen interest and apply yourself. Some of the most learned Bible scholars taught themselves, by the aid of the Holy Spirit, because they were intensely interested in finding out everything they could about God's Word.

If you do not have a great curiosity about the Bible, ask the Lord to give you a hunger and thirst for His Word.

49

They Found Fault

Can you imagine anyone finding fault with the
Lord Jesus Christ? Well, Mark tells us that when the
Pharisees saw Jesus' disciples eating with unwashen
hands, "they found fault" (Mk 7:2*b*). At that time
Jesus had been performing miracles of healing, but the
Pharisees were not looking for that.

The spirit of pharisaism can mark even Bible-be-
lieving Christians. A Christian can become exceedingly
critical of others, even about the gospel. Bible students
are sometimes notorious for "splitting hairs," that is,
they make issues out of small matters; "mountains out
of molehills."

A critical spirit is an attitude of judging, and judgment should be left to Jesus alone. The Pharisees
thought they could judge who was spiritual and who
was not. Only God knows the heart; therefore, only
He can rightly judge.

A mountaineer was shooting snakes in an area where
stones, logs, stream, and foliage all seemed to be the
same color. Yet, the sharpshooter never failed to see
the slightest part of a snake that showed.

"How do you do it?" someone asked.

"I get the color in my eye," he said. "Then I look
for that color and nothing else. It's what you look
for."

99

The same is true with people. What you look for is what you see. If you look for faults, that is what you will see. If you look for that which is praiseworthy, that is what you will see.

How rarely people are helped by being criticized, but how often they are inspired by honest commendation. From your own experience you know that encouragement has helped you much more than fault-finding.

The Lord Jesus never condemned the sinner but forgave him. He sometimes complimented persons who had not yet come to believe in Him. Before Nathanael met Jesus he was very skeptical and said, "Can any good thing come out of Nazareth?" When Philip brought him to Jesus, the Lord said of him, "Behold, an Israelite in whom is no guile."

Even when sinners rejected Him, the Lord continued to love them. The rich young ruler wanted Jesus, but he could not part with his possessions. Looking upon him, the Lord loved him. When the young man went away sorrowfully, no doubt our Lord's eyes followed him with the same loving-kindness with which He had welcomed him.

Very often we judge others by ourselves. That is, we suspect others of being guilty of what we ourselves are guilty of. The Lord commands, "Don't criticize people, and you will not be criticized. For you will be judged by the way you criticize others, and the measure you give will be the measure you receive" (Mt 7:1-2a, Phillips).

50

Bit and Bridle

In the spring of the year, when the grass is yet young and tender, find a pasture where horses graze in the sun. There are the mares with their colts, wobbly on tall, spindly legs; the bays, sorrels, buckskin, paints, palominos; the Shetlands, the quarter horses, the Tennessee Walking Horses; the stallions—any of them make a beautiful sight.

Those young colts nuzzling their mothers are lovely to look at, but they will be worthless unless they are broken to bit and bridle when they mature. Sometimes the process is not difficult if the colts have been treated well and loved. Otherwise, it takes force and patience. Yet the wildest horse can be tamed if properly handled.

James spoke of putting bits in horses' mouths to control them. He was illustrating the fact that although the bit and bridle are small compared to the horse, they are the controlling factors.

Have you ever said something and then felt guilty about it? Have you ever wished that you had kept your mouth shut? If you haven't, your conscience must have been hardened because James tells us, "The man who can claim that he never says the wrong thing can consider himself perfect, for if he can control his tongue he can control every other part of his personality!" (Ja 3:2, Phillips). He tells us that every kind of wild beast can be tamed, "but no human being can tame the tongue. It is always ready to pour out its deadly poison" (Ja 3:8, Living NT).

What then? Are we the victims of this little member of the body? Is there no escape?

David was aware of how unruly the tongue can be, so he called upon the Lord, praying, "Set a watch, O LORD, before my mouth; keep the door of my lips" (Ps 141:3). Nevertheless, David knew that he must do his part, and in another psalm he wrote, "I am purposed that my mouth shall not transgress" (Ps 17:3).

The temptation to talk too freely is a very strong temptation. What is written in the Scripture concerning our tongues and the use of them? Words "fitly spoken" are "like apples of gold in pictures of silver" (Pr 25:11b).

There are hundreds of verses in the Bible to strengthen your resolve to overcome this temptation. You may find them by using a concordance. Store them in your memory for ready use.

Look at your own life and see how and when you use your tongue in disobedience to God. When you wake up, let your first prayer be for help along this line as you face that temptation. If you are prepared to meet it and you are on your guard against it, you may take the offense against the misuse of your tongue by making positive statements to turn the tide of conversation. Instead of enjoying abusive speech, begin to enjoy upbuilding others with what you say.

102

51

Food

Teenagers are notorious for the quantity of food they can consume. A family was planning an afternoon of activity. The parents were going to the beach, the relatives to town, and the little children to the creek to fish. The sixteen-year-old brother was quite serious when he said, "I believe I'll stay home and eat."

He did too! When the family returned, the boy was lying on the couch. A nearby stack of plates and several empty glasses and pop bottles were evidence of his favorite pastime.

Mothers sometimes complain that growing boys and girls will hardly finish a meal before they are raiding the refrigerator for snacks.

Probably you are nagged about eating too much sugar or drinking too many bottles of pop, etc. Maybe you have suffered the consequences of your indulging —a terrible stomachache or toothache in the middle of the night and perhaps a trip to the doctor or dentist.

Your body requires the proper type of food and a certain quantity when you are growing rapidly. It is important that you eat enough and that you eat the right things.

Daniel was a teenager when he was taken captive to

Babylon. He and his friends were selected to be trained in the king's court for future work in the government. A part of their duty was to eat at the king's table.

The boys took one look at all that food and they knew that they had a decision to make. Many of the foods, such as pork, were forbidden by God to the Hebrews at that time. Also, the heathen king served strong drink.

Daniel requested permission to eat plain, ordinary food. The request was granted on an experimental condition. If the boys stayed in good health on the diet, they could continue eating their own food.

It isn't hard to guess that they fared better than the boys who ate the rich food. The boys who stuffed themselves with fats, sweets, and starches must not have felt like studying when dinner was over. They felt sluggish and sleepy (if they didn't have heartburn). The wine made them dizzy and their minds did not function well.

Daniel and his friends were like athletes in training who avoid fattening foods. They were in good condition for study or for exercise.

Your body is the temple of the living God. Do you keep His temple in the best of condition by proper diet?

52

Man or Puppet?

A puppet is a mechanical toy which operates under the control of a person. Some Christians expect God to treat them as puppets, giving them special direction for every move that they make. They want God to think for them, decide for them. Sometimes such an attitude paralyzes a Christian so that he will not move in any direction for fear of moving in the wrong way.

God often gives us general orders and then we proceed accordingly. "The integrity of the upright shall guide them" (Pr 11:3). "The righteousness of the perfect shall direct his way" (Pr 11:5; cf. 3:23; 6:20-22; 10:9). Godly principles are like the multiplication tables. Every time you work a math problem you do not consciously think of the multiplication tables, do you? As God's Word is hidden in the heart, we are able to make righteous judgments along the way without demanding that God make decisions for us in special ways.

Jesus told His disciples that they were expected to go beyond the call of duty in serving Him. He gave them an illustration of servants who had fulfilled their specific requirements, and asked, "Do you feel particularly grateful to your servant for doing what you tell him? I don't think so. It is the same with yourselves—when you have done everything that you are told to do, you can say, 'We are not much good as servants, for we have only done what we ought to do' " (Lk 17:9-10, Phillips) .

If your mother had a servant would she want to have to tell the woman every table to dust, every corner to mop? Of course not; she would say, "This room is to be cleaned." A good servant knows what to do and an especially good servant would add finishing touches that you might not classify as her duty. Such a servant would be in line for special commendation.

The apostle Paul received his general orders to be a missionary to the Gentiles. He proceeded accordingly. One time he started to go into Bithynia but God intervened and told him to go to Macedonia instead. This illustrates the principle that a Christian is to proceed according to the integrity of his heart, according to the uprightness of his character as one completely dedicated to the glory of God, knowing that God will direct his paths. Each day must be committed to the Lord in faith.

Only ignorance of God's Word or a lack of trust in Him will keep a Christian going around in circles, indecisive and miserable. To get out of such a situation, begin by reading God's Word and obeying the general orders and the simple commands.

53

Fears

Nearly everyone has a slightly abnormal fear about something. Such fears are called phobias. There is the fear of high places called "acrophobia," and the fear of being closed in, "claustrophobia." There are phobias about animals, germs, and a thousand other things.

Psychologists can explain why we have these fears and they can suggest remedies that will help if carried out. Severe fear can be torture, and a person should seek help to be relieved. A pastor or teacher can help or put you in touch with someone who can help.

But there is immediate help for you from the Word of God if you are a Christian. The Bible is full of "Fear nots." If you will look them up in a concordance, and then apply them personally, you will be helped. Take, for instance, the fear of death: "The LORD is my shepherd; . . . I will fear no evil" (Ps 23:1-4).

Perhaps you have a rather normal fear of the unknown. Imagine that you have never undergone surgery and that you are scheduled for an operation in the morning. Isaiah 41:10 will help you: "Fear thou not; for I *am* with thee: be not dismayed; for I *am* thy God: I will strengthen thee; yea, I will help thee; yea,

I will uphold thee with the right hand of my right-eousness." Take this as a promise of the Lord to you.

Memorize these verses about fear so that you can use them in emergencies when a Bible is not available. You can help others too by recalling the verses when they are experiencing difficulties.

It helps to read about men of God who were faced with danger and to learn how the Lord helped them.

When Jehoshaphat was faced with invasion from Moab, he "feared, and set himself to seek the LORD, and proclaimed a fast throughout all Judah" (2 Ch 20:3). The result of their seeking the Lord was that Jehoshaphat acknowledged their inability to defend themselves: "For we have no might against this great company that cometh against us; neither know we what to do: but our eyes *are* upon thee" (2 Ch 20:12).

Then the people of Judah went forth to battle, singing and praising God, because God's prophet had assured them of victory even though they wouldn't have to fight. When the praise began, the victory began! (2 Ch 20:22-24).

Great men of God have shared your fears. Jeremiah complained of stage fright, but God commanded him not to be "afraid of their faces" (Jer 1:8).

Begin your project of overcoming fears by learning Psalm 56:3, "What time I am afraid, I will trust in thee."

54

Fear and Faith

Shadrach, Meshach, and Abednego were faced with the cruelest punishment if they did not bow down to Nebuchadnezzar's image. They would be thrown into a roaring fire to be burned alive.

Put yourself in their shoes. Would you relish the agony of flames licking at your flesh? Of course not, and neither did they! They were as human as you are! And they probably were teenagers. They had never heard of God delivering anyone thrown into a fire. Although they knew He was able, they had little hope that He would.

When the king offered them a second chance to escape the fire, they could have held a conference and decided to compromise. But they didn't! They replied, "The God whom we serve is able to save us from the fire of the furnace and He will deliver *us* out of your hand, O king" (Dan 3:17, Berkeley). They knew that if they died in the flames they would be delivered from the cruel king. They would win—one way or the other. They were not afraid to make the claim for God that He could keep them from the flames. "But, whether He does or not, be it known to you, O king, we will not serve your gods, or worship the image which you have set up" (Dan 3:18, Berkeley).

They were definite in their decision. Acting upon that which was right, they left the consequences to God. Afraid? Yes, to a limited degree, but not afraid of the eternal results of their action.

You must settle it in your mind that you will act upon the principles laid down in God's Word—even if it should cost you your life. The time may come when you will be faced with just such a choice. You need not think that you will pass the final test if you fail in the small things in life. How easy it is to think that we would lay down our lives for the Lord, but if we will not yield in the little things in everyday life, what makes us so sure that we would be faithful if a major crisis occurs?

If we can act upon principle day by day, regardless of the ridicule or misunderstanding that might come our way, it stands to reason that we will be better prepared to stand the greater tests.

The Hebrew boys were saved by a miracle, but many Christians have been burned for their faith. God does not always choose to deliver us from bodily harm, but He has promised not to let us be tempted more than we are able to bear. "To him that overcometh" God makes glorious promises (Rev 2:7, 11, 17, 26; 3:5, 12, 21).

55

Living in a Scientific Age

In the space age we can't escape the dominance of science in our lives. However, we are not the only generation that has witnessed rapid advancement in technology and discovery.

The Babylonians were scientists of rank. The intellectual climate of the palace was such that young men were recruited to dedicate their entire time to learning the wisdom of the sages.

Among the young scholars was a conquered Israelite who was brought to the palace as a teenager. His name was Daniel.

Like Moses, who learned from the Egyptians, Daniel listened to everything that was taught. No doubt he was exposed to the mysticism of astrology, to the growing theories of the universe, to the legal writings of Babylonian lawyers.

God gave Daniel holy discernment to discriminate between the true and the false. His refusal to eat foods forbidden to the Jews might have resulted in censure or rejection; nevertheless, Daniel honored God and God honored Daniel.

Daniel did not compromise the truth when he predicted the future, even if his prediction contained judgment for the kings to whom he prophesied.

When ordered to bow down to an image, upon pain of death, he refused and steadfastly prayed to the living God.

Daniel far surpassed his fellow scholars in learning and ability, and was recognized repeatedly by the Babylonian government. He even rose in rank second to the king!

What God did for Daniel He can do for you today. Do not be afraid of learning. All truth, whether it is in the field of science, language, or history, is from God. Furthermore, the Lord will give you discernment, as He did Daniel, to differentiate between truth and error.

Daniel's testimony is based on his continual communication with God through prayer (three times a day). Other captives gave up hope, but Daniel read the writings of the prophet Jeremiah and found hope in his prediction that the captivity would end in seventy years.

God can make a Daniel out of you if you will yield your intellect to Him and let Him lead you into all truth. The intellectual circles of this world may be hostile to the living God and you may risk some sort of twentieth-century "lions' den," but if you honor God then He will honor you.

56

New Mexico Mine

Socorro, New Mexico, is a very old town, built by the Spaniards in the early 1600s. A vein of rich silver had been discovered in the bleak-looking hills.

Today you can visit the San Miquel Church that was built in Socorro in 1638. Once it was lavishly decorated with silver ornaments and vessels, but today it is a plain, bare building.

The silver mine brought a thriving community to Socorro. Many men found work and some found wealth in the operation. But today the mine is closed. People in Socorro work in other occupations. The population decreased when the people moved away a long time ago.

I knew a good man who was kind and gentle. For thirty-five years, under all kinds of circumstances, his virtues seemed constant. They were like a rich vein of ore providing spiritual wealth for his family and friends.

Then, kindness faltered, gentleness failed. Like the rich vein of silver in the Socorro mine, the "ore" ran out. No amount of probing and digging revealed the slightest trace of his former goodness.

What had happened to the man? A "root of bitterness" was in his heart and he did not pull it out. It grew until it strangled him spiritually. He became a bitter old man.

Any root of bitterness which you allow to continue will finally win out. Get rid of any unforgiving spirit —a grudge or jealousy.

Sometimes worldliness crowds out the virtues of the Holy Spirit. Soon the "gold" of righteousness, the "platinum" of integrity, and the "ruby" of humility are scorned for the "brass" of self-security, the "chrome" of comforts, the "rust" of plenty.

Psychologists often blame ailments and attitudes upon childhood experiences. Murders, suicides, alcoholism, drug addiction, and other tragic results have been traced to harmful experiences which an individual had while growing up.

Even a Christian may not recognize all the reasons behind his actions, but he can avoid many bad results if he will look over his experience and then root out wrong attitudes that have piled up. At the present you may be able to "live on top" of your unfortunate experiences, but unless you root out bitterness, grudges, jealousy, etc., you will suffer the loss of a full and rich Christian experience.

When you reach old age, will your life be a rich source of blessing to others, or will the goodness you now enjoy be swallowed up by the wrong?

57

Fort Moultrie

At the beginning of the Revolutionary War, Colonel Moultrie was assigned the task of defending the city of Charleston, South Carolina. A fort was needed to defend the harbor, but the conventional building materials (stone or oak) were not available. Colonel Moultrie decided to use a double-wall construction of the only material available, the spongy, soft palmetto tree. Everyone thought the fort would give way with the first attack of cannon.

Sir Peter Parker, the British naval officer in charge of the attack, led the onslaught. As the men-of-war approached the island, all nine ships fired simultaneously. The volley fell short but the next round found its range. The cannonballs struck the fort inside and out, but there was no splintering of wood, no crashing of walls! When the militia investigated, they found the iron balls stuck in the soft wood without damage. The siege continued all day, but the fort absorbed the punishment and the militia was enabled to inflict damage to the enemy. When the British fleet withdrew, the flagship dipped its flag in salute to the gallant fort and its men.

Many a Christian has found that the "softness" of his character—his tenderness, meekness, patience, and

115

self-control—has enabled him to absorb all that the enemy of souls can inflict. It is not likely that Satan will salute the Christian who withstands his assaults, but we may be sure that the Lord is pleased.

The Bible tells us, "A soft answer turneth away wrath" (Pr 15:1a), and Satan is dumbfounded when one of God's children stops a quarrel in the beginning by giving a "soft" answer. The "defense of the faith" takes all kinds of "forts"—all kinds of strong character traits.

58

Welcome to America

Emma Lazarus was a Jewish poetess. When the Statue of Liberty was erected on Liberty Island in New York harbor, she was asked to submit a manuscript to be sold to raise money for the base of the statue. She wrote the famous lines which are now written on a plaque inside the base of the statue.

> Give me your tired, your poor,
> Your huddled masses yearning to breathe free,
> The wretched refuse of your teeming shore,
> Send these, the homeless, tempest-tossed, to me,
> I lift my lamp beside the golden door!

General George C. Marshall once said that if he had his way, the lady would hold, instead of a lamp, an open Bible.

An open Bible does make for liberty. On the Liberty Bell in Philadelphia our forefathers had a text from Leviticus inscribed: "Proclaim liberty throughout the land" (Lev 25:10).

Both our Christian ideals and our democratic ideals espouse the cause of the poor and oppressed. Do you, as an individual, espouse the same ideals in your personal relationships? In other words, do you show hospitality toward strangers or young people less fortunate than yourself? Do you respect the rights of others, or are you prejudiced against others having the freedom that you enjoy?

The Lord told Moses to remember to show hospitality to strangers and He reminded His people that they were once strangers in Egypt.

The new person in your community, your school, or church, is a stranger. It is your opportunity and privilege to make him feel welcome. If you have ever been in a new community you know how important it is to be accepted and befriended.

59

The Shrine of Democracy

Gutzon Borglum, the artist who carved the likenesses of four Presidents on Mount Rushmore, envisioned his work long before he was enabled to accomplish it. He wrote, "I want, somewhere in America on or near the Rockies, the backbone of the Continent, far removed from succeeding, selfish, coveting civilizations, a few feet of stone that bears witness, carries the likenesses, the dates, a word or two of the great things we accomplished as a Nation, placed so high it won't pay to pull down for lesser purposes."

In the Black Hills of South Dakota such a piece of stone was found, a granite mountain that reached the clouds. The specific Presidents chosen to epitomize the American ideal were men who served the nation during times of crisis. Washington represents the struggle for liberty when the republic was founded. Jefferson expresses the nation's democratic philosophy. Lincoln embodies the preservation of the Union. Theodore Roosevelt represents expansion and conservation of the country's natural resources.

Every American has a sense of deep gratitude to God when he sees the faces of these men who represent the history of this country. In the providence of God they guided the ship of state to make it the greatest nation in the world.

As popular as it is to make uncomplimentary remarks about America, it is far more fitting to offer prayers of thanksgiving for its past and to ask the Lord to correct it where it is wrong in order to preserve a free society. What God has done in the past for "this nation under God," He is able to do in the future. He promises, "If my people which are called by my name, shall humble themselves, and pray, and seek my face, and turn from their wicked ways; then will I hear from heaven, and will forgive their sin, and will heal their land" (2 Ch 7:14). God does not call upon the unbeliever to rejuvenate the spiritual life of a nation, but He calls upon His own people.

Isn't it a wonderful truth that you, as an ordinary citizen, may have as important a role in the nation's history as the man who knelt at Valley Forge; or the one who wrote about man's God-given rights; or the one who sought to "heal a nation's wounds" with "malice toward none and charity toward all"; or the one who sought to reform public morals?

The prayers of John Knox broke the power of oppression in Scotland. Prayer can preserve this nation too.

60

Christmas Holidays

How eagerly we look forward to the holidays before and after Christmas. The days off from school seem to offer ample time for all the things we need or want to do. Yet, when the time comes, we are often busier than ever and do not accomplish all that we had planned to do.

When vacation begins, do the truly important things first. How easy it is to relax first and then run out of time for the necessary things.

If you have a job, you will not have very much time off, but you will have extra money. Put "first things first" with regard to your money. When we have additional money, we have a tendency to overspend or to go in debt. The discipline of a budget will insure that you keep your expenditures within reason.

Since these are holy days and not merely holidays, the things of Christ should have top priority in your plans. The tendency is to become overly active in projects of charity so that true worship is crowded out. If anything, your personal communion with Christ should have extended sessions of prayer and study of God's Word. If you have free time, read additional literature concerning the birth of our Lord. Search your church library for appropriate books and magazines.

Television is a particular temptation at Christmastime because of the colorful programs presented in the festive atmosphere of the season. Some of these programs can be time thieves. Even "good" programs can be the enemy of the best use of time.

Christmas vacation is a time for reviewing the past and looking forward to the future. As Jesus came the first time, so He has promised to return. Perhaps He will come before next Christmas Eve.

61

New Year's Eve

How many times have you celebrated New Year's Eve? How many more do you think you might celebrate? This is a sobering question.

The psalmist said, "The days of our years are three-score years and ten; and if by reason of strength they be fourscore years, yet is their strength labour and sorrow; for it is soon cut off, and we fly away" (Ps 90:10). It is thought that this is the oldest psalm in the Bible. It is all about the brevity of life and the eternity of God.

It is difficult for young people to think of the brevity of life because few young people die. Psychologically, we feel as if we shall have many years to live and have plenty of time to be what we should be and do what we should do.

There is an old adage that applies: "The old must die, the young may die." But, what if you do live to be seventy or eighty years old—is there ever enough time to do all the interesting things you would like to do? You have probably entertained ideas of various careers—if you followed all of them, you would need several lives.

Perhaps you remember Dr. Tom Dooley, the young doctor who founded Medico, a medical mission to people in Southeast Asia, five miles from the Communist border. He was hardly out of his twenties when it was discovered that he had cancer. Shortly before he died, he wrote his autobiography. The title of his book came from one of Robert Frost's poems, "... *and I have miles to go before I sleep.*"

Tom Dooley did not travel many miles farther before his life was snuffed out.

You may have miles to go before you "sleep." If your life is to count for the Lord Jesus Christ, you must open your heart to His leading.

62

Summer Plans

What will you do when you get out of school for the summer? All kinds of ideas must be popping into your head for getting the most out of those weeks. Your biggest dreams might be schemes to take you abroad. Or maybe you are planning to get a job to earn some money.

If you are at a loss to know how you might realize some of these possibilities, check with your principal, guidance counselor, or teacher. Libraries often have material available that will put you in touch with the right people.

If you need a job, begin now to apply. Read the want ads, apply to the employment bureau, or write to government agencies.

Perhaps your denomination sponsors fieldwork for teenagers on mission fields during the summer. You may get work in a Christian camp or Bible conference. Ask your pastor or youth director for information.

Staying at home can be exciting too. (The grass always seems greener on the other side of the fence!) In your own home there are opportunities for learning, recreation, and service if you will take the time to find them.

The most important factor in making this a profitable summer is to plan ahead. Measure the time you have by the things you want to accomplish. If you wish to read certain books, schedule them so that you will make sure to get them all in. If you need a certain amount of money by next fall, budget what you will earn and discipline yourself to save the necessary amount.

Perhaps you want to learn a skill—to play tennis, to sew or cook, to drive, to play a guitar. Take advantage of the time you will have in the summer to enjoy the available opportunities.

With more free time you can devote more attention to those whom you can help. A younger brother or sister may need your special interest at this time. Grandparents and other elderly people will appreciate your cheerful helpfulness. Do some special things for others, not because you have to but because you want to.

A daughter once teasingly chided her mother, "Mom, what are you going to do when you reach heaven and the Lord asks you why you gave away everything He gave you?"

The mother replied, "I'll just say, 'Lord, that's all I brought with me—the things I gave away.' "

Let your summer be not only a time of enrichment for yourself but a time when you give away some of what the Lord has given you.

63

Commencement

All over the country the months of May and June are marked by graduations. A graduation means an end to a period of schooling. A graduate looks back with fond memories of happy associations and with regrets that he did not do better or differently. But graduation is not an end—it is a beginning, a *commencement*. For some it is the commencement of a career, a home, or further schooling.

Throughout life you will experience "graduations" and "commencements"—not that you will continually be receiving diplomas, but you will reach the end of one experience and will enter another phase of experience.

For the Christian, the Bible says that every day is a graduation and a commencement, for "the path of the just is as a shining light, that shineth more and more unto the perfect day" (Pr 4:18).

No condition in life remains for long. If you are experiencing sorrow, soon the cycle will bring you around to joy; and vice versa. It is well to be prepared for life's graduations.

The disciples refused to believe Jesus when He told them that He would be crucified and then rise again on the third day, so they were not prepared. When the crucifixion was accomplished, they thought it was the end.

But the most glorious commencement in the history of the world took place when Jesus was raised from the dead. The disciples thought they would then have Christ as their king, as He lived among them for another forty days.

But there was another "graduation," for He ascended into heaven. This time they seemed better prepared for the approaching commencement. When the Holy Spirit manifested Himself ten days later on the day of Pentecost, the evangelization of the world began. There is never an ending but what there is a beginning!